Dream Job!!!
A Strengths Based Guide To Finding Work You Love

A SUCCESSPATH SERIES BOOK

DALE COBB

Published by Career Media, a division of SUCCESSPATH Career Development, Inc.

Career Media books may be purchased in bulk for educational, business, fundraising, or sales promotional use.

Library of Congress Cataloging-in-Publication Data

Cobb, Dale, 1957-

 Dream Job!!! – A Strengths Based Guide To Finding Work You Love / Dale Cobb

ISBN-10: 1548681385
ISBN-13: 978-1548681388

DEDICATION

Thank you to my parents,

Allen and Frances Cobb

who always encouraged me

to pursue my dreams…

And to my beautiful wife and editor

Susy who stood by me when

that wasn't going so well.

CONTENTS

READ THIS FIRST!

The purpose of this book is to help you rock your job search!

Job Search is one of the most difficult activities many people encounter and it's getting more complicated. The *Boyer Management Group* believes there is more than 2100 job search best practices.

One mission of *SUCCESSPATH* is to teach modern job search strategies and skills in a supportive environment to the unemployed. I say modern because job search is changing rapidly. Classic job search methods that worked for decades are now dated relics of a past era. But sometimes older practices actually prove more effective than their contemporary counterparts. I blend the classic with the contemporary, always staying focused on what works. This may mean teaching an older worker how to build a resume that will make it through applicant tracking software. Or it may mean teaching a younger worker how to bypass online applications and go out to properly introduce themselves.

In 2011, 88% of those who graduated or completed the *SUCCESSPATH Road to Jobs* two week program found work in an average of 10 days. The graduates did this in an environment that *USA Today* called "the 5th hardest place to find work in America".

I help clients prepare for an effective job search by engaging them in Strengths Clarification, Targeting Roles, Resume Writing and Interview Preparation. Then I help them execute a four path job search. This includes Direct Contact into the Hidden Job Market, applying to Employer Postings, engaging in Relationship Networking and using Staffing and Search firms. I now help them get organized with a simplified *Agile* methodology used by some of the most successful companies in the world.

Some of the jobs the clients get are Platform Jobs or Springboard Jobs that begin to provide basic financial resources. But *SUCCESSPATH* has a much bigger mission. I teach career development strategies designed to maximize clients' talent and passion, optimize performance and increase contribution. The end result should be increased success, satisfaction and a better pay check!

Once a client has found a job, I love to continue working with them on ways to deliver the best of themselves.

The training begins with the following questions:
What do you naturally do best?
What do you love doing?
How can you deliver that in the workplace?

But those questions are not what most people use to select a career.

According to *Deloitte Consulting*, 65% of U.S. workers are planning to leave their current employer.

According to a 2010 *Manpower Group* survey, 5 out of 6 adults in North America are considering changing their jobs.

A *Harris Interactive* poll of 7,718 workers said:
42% feel burnt out
33% feel dead ended (They see no future in their job.)
85% do not feel strongly energized by their work

Franklin Covey polled 23,000 workers finding that:

    80% of employees feel unenthusiastic about their goals

    50% feel dissatisfied with their work at the end of the week

Gallup's data regularly suggests that less than 20% of us get to use our strengths on a daily basis at work.

Nicholas Lore is the author of *The Pathfinder* and co-author of *What Now*. Nick has received accommodations for his work from two U.S. Presidents for helping over 14,000 individuals make career transitions. He estimates **30% see their work as a negative** to the point of being dysfunctional or disruptive. Another **10% actually may be dangerous**.

If you're interested in learning how to identify and get the job of your dreams, keep reading!

Prologue

Why Strengths?

Multiple studies have confirmed the importance of strengths as a foundation for career selection. One, a 7-year study of 197,000 individuals across 23 countries performed by *Innermetrix*, revealed the two defining factors that differentiated top performers from the moderate and low performers.

These two factors were self-awareness and authenticity.

Awareness: This is an accurate understanding of what you are not good at, and perhaps just as importantly, what you **are** good at. The average level of self-awareness was 57% across the study. The highest performers (called the Genius level), typically had a 90% self-awareness rating.

Authenticity: This is a measure of how true or aligned you are to your self-awareness. A high level of authenticity means you do what you are good at, and don't do what you are bad at. The top performers had a 90% level of authenticity.

The good news is that these two factors can be developed. With some work on self-awareness, and some focus on authenticity, **we all have potential for Genius performance.**

Benefits of Working From Your Strengths

High Performance

Gallup studies show business units with employees who, do what they do best everyday, outperform in at least 10 categories.

Working from your natural strengths is **the only way** you will ever become **WORLD CLASS!**

World-class performers **out earn moderate and good performers** in almost every field. They sometimes earn more exponentially.

World-class performers always have work. **They are never laid off.**

Satisfaction and Fulfillment

Performing in roles that utilize your natural talents help you find a sense of satisfaction that you don't get when you are forced to work from a non-talent.

The Real You - Self Acceptance

Your natural talent based role is of great importance. Many people get to experience that "it's okay to be me" feeling for the first time when they begin working from their strengths.

Natural Energy

Working from your strengths opens up great reservoirs of natural energy. Working from a non-talent is usually draining both emotionally and physically.

Focus and Boundaries

Knowing with certainty what you do best, allows you to focus your life. It gives you the confidence and rationale to say no to an opportunity that doesn't play to your strengths.

Harmony at Work

Communicating your strengths at work allows others to know you better. Understanding the strengths of others allows you to appreciate them at a deeper level and maximizes team work.

BONUS - Family Communications

When you get the career piece right, it's much easier to build a great family and marriage. Unemployment and working in a career that doesn't fit are both hard on a marriage and your children. Beyond that, the most basic of all human needs is to be understood. Grasping the strengths of your spouse and your children will take you a long way down the path of understanding.

BONUS – Better Health

The happier you are at work, the healthier you'll likely be.

Company Benefits

If you think you might want to work in management someday, your ability to hire great people and get them in positions that fit their unique strengths is a huge plus for any employer.

Simply put, employees who work from their strengths contribute more to the organization!

Gallup studied 32,393 business/work units, including 955,905 employees, while looking closely at 10 business outcomes. They found an extremely high correlation with worker engagement and employees who were placed in positions where they could work from their strengths.

12% higher customer service metrics

18% higher productivity

16% higher profitability

37% lower absenteeism

25% lower turnover In high turnover organizations

49% lower turnover in low turnover organizations

27% less theft

49% fewer safety accidents

41% fewer "patient" safety accidents

60% fewer quality defects

The *SUCCESSPATH* **mission is** to radically increase the percentage of people in the world who "**Do What They Do Best**" every single day. We want to help you become the **Best Version of Yourself**. Right now, according to *Gallup*, that number is well under 20%. That means over 80% of our workforce isn't fulfilling its performance potential or its enjoyment potential.

Another way to state our mission is that *SUCCESSPATH* exists to help you:

Discover what you do best using your natural contributive advantage

Describe/Demonstrate what you do best and communicate it clearly

Develop what you do best with complimentary skills and knowledge

Deliver what you do best in the work you love

Dial It In by refining and improving what you do best forever

There is no magic wand or formula in this book. There are only field tested strategies, which, when mixed with your own hard work, will produce good results. And job search is hard work! For many, it is harder work than going to school. For most, it will be harder than the day to day tasks of the work you are seeking.

This may also be different than other searches you have conducted. It could be the first time you've actually conducted a "professional job search". As you move into the professional world, you will have to step up your game. If it's been a few years, job search may have changed drastically.

My purpose is to make your job search process:

1. Easier - Maybe not easy, but easier
2. Effective
3. Faster
4. More Fun

In my workshops, I often begin by asking, **"What are the characteristics of people who get jobs? What makes them different?"**

I usually get answers like training, education, skills, experience and knowledge. These are all true and good answers. But the answer is woefully incomplete. Richard Bolles personally helped over 40,000 individuals find jobs. He was the author of *What Color Is Your Parachute,* the best-selling job search book of all time. Bolles said, **"The people who get jobs are not always the most qualified. The people who get jobs are the people who know how to get jobs."** Bolles was right. And they often have a better sense of what hiring managers look for.

What Hiring Managers Look For

There are 8 primary reasons candidates get hired. I call this the "A-Game of Job Search".

Awareness - Focus on the employers' perspective. Many job candidates are only thinking about themselves and what they want. The candidate who walks in focusing on the employer's concern has a big advantage.

Adding Value - It's common for a job search candidate to believe they are being hired for a set of skills. But we are all hired to add value, make a specific contribution or realize a result. Millions of ¼" drill bits are sold each year. But what those buyers are really wanting is a ¼" hole.

Ability – Average employers ask the question, "Can this person do the job? Do they have the skills and knowledge?" Great employers ask, "Does this person have the appetite or affinity for this job? Do they have the aptitudes that will allow them to learn new skills quickly and easily? Will they love the day-to-day activities of the job?"

Attitude – All employers look for positive attitudes. Is the job candidate likeable? Will they fit in? Will they be easy to get along with? Will they build others up or tear them down? What shows up when they walk in the room?

Ambition – Does the candidate want to learn and grow? Or will they just go through the motions? Great companies like *Apple,* tend to look for people who want to grow and expand in the role they are being hired for, rather than work their way to other positions.

Appearance – Smart companies are building a brand reputation and a culture. They are looking for a look that will advance that brand and reputation.

Attendance – All employers are looking for workers who keep their commitments. This means being available to work, showing up and showing up a few minutes early.

Associates – Many employers consider who you hang out with. In some cases they look for the type of activities you engage in during your off hours. Some employers look for existing business alliances that will benefit the organization.

For a deeper dive into some of these issues, I recommend *The 6 Reasons You'll Get the Job* by Debra L. Angel & Elisabeth H. Sanders-Park.

In this book, I will focus on **Set Up Steps, 4 Job Search Preparation Steps** and **4 Job Search Execution Steps.** I introduce a conversation on Job Search Challenges, Job Shaping and offer a section on what I call Job Search Jazz. I then conclude with an introduction to *Agile* Project Management with an application to job search.

Professional Set Up Steps

Professional email address and checking messages daily.
Professional voice mail, checking daily, keeping box empty.
Professional image and wardrobe.
Keep all appointments always arriving 10 minutes early.
Communicate positivity and professionalism at all times.
Conduct Information Interviews with hiring managers.

Job Search "Preparation" Steps

Step 1: Clarify your **Stand-Out Strengths and Selling Points** including passion, talent, skills, knowledge, transferrable experience and how each can contribute to an employer.

Step 2: Turn your strengths into **Targets** with a Professional Objective Statement, Target Market Statement, an A-B-C-D Target Sheet and have a working list of 50-100 potential employers.

Step 3: Create a **Resume Package** that includes a customizable master resume, cover letter, portfolio, reference, endorsement and leave-behind sheets.

Step 4: Coordinate **Interview Preparation** with company research, written talking points, appropriate clothing and thank you notes.

Job Search "Execution" Steps

Step 5: Put together a **Direct Contact** strategy approaching employers for hidden or un-posted jobs.

Step 6: Check *Craigslist* and *Indeed* for **Employer Postings** and then apply online in the most effective way possible.

Step 7: Start a **Relationship Networking** campaign connecting with people working in your targeted career. Look for and join industry groups, attend meetings and maximize social media platforms like *LinkedIn*.

Step 8: Register with **Search and Staffing** companies.

Other Job Search Considerations

The 8 steps listed above comprise the heart of the system. But here are some additional areas covered in the book:

Identifying and managing job search **Challenges**.

Maximizing today's job while preparing to **Shift** into your next role.

Shaping your new job to fit your strengths.

Improvising and swinging with **Job Search Jazz**.

Executing the *Agile* **Job Search Project** system including the Kanban Board, Sprint, Sprint Plan, Sprint Review and Sprint Retrospective.

SUCCESS 101 - GETTING SET UP

Foundations

There are a few universal principles that successful people use to maximize success in any endeavor. Achievers constantly work on their mindset, attitude and focus on the things they can control. **The most effective individuals take full responsibility for their success.** They create flexible plans and take massive action. Strong candidates view job search as a full-time commitment. They structure their time. If they don't have an environment that is conducive to getting work done, they go to the library, a campus or one of many *America's Job Center* sites. Successful candidates carefully follow a sequenced, well-crafted, proven job search strategy like the one in this book.

Job Search Dips, Distractions and Ditches

The most effective job search candidates recognize that everyone has barriers and roadblocks. Top candidates study their own barriers and utilize strategies that will allow them to re-route, climb over, go around or tunnel underneath. Successful candidates spend little time whining and complaining and more time trying to identify solutions.

Many people stay in jobs that are well below their potential because they either dislike job search or have never developed the skills. Part of maximizing your potential is becoming effective at looking for new work.

Structure

Many job searches fail for lack of a well sequenced, well organized strategy as summarized at the end of the Prologue. But many also fail for lack of a structured place to carry out that search. When candidates lose a job, graduate or get out of the military, they all have one thing in common. They just lost their structure. They don't have anyone to report to. They don't have anyone to tell them what to do or where to go. They are thrust into an environment where they have to make it up and make it happen. Some of us don't come from backgrounds where we have a lot of experience doing this.

Part of the *SUCCESSPATH* **SECRET SAUCE** is providing a structure. Having a place to go to work and someone to report to makes all the difference. Zig Ziglar used to share - no one makes it to the top of Mount Everest by going out and wandering around. A successful career doesn't happen that way either. It's a very intentional process. There are strategies that consistently work, strategies that occasionally work and strategies that rarely work. Most job seekers focus on strategies that occasionally or rarely work.

Set up a schedule and a makeshift office at the library, a campus or one of *America's Job Center* sites. Get an accountability coach. Go to work every day on a regular schedule.

Don't move through this section too quickly. I know you have job search challenges and barriers. You are too young or too old. You have too little experience, too little of the right experience or too much experience. There are dozens of common job search barriers or challenges. Just about everyone falls into one category and many face multiple barriers. Most of us hallucinate that our situation is uniquely dreadful and others are having an easier go of it than we are.

Mindset Matters!

I've worked with hundreds of individuals on job search and hundreds more on other areas of career development. **The most common barrier or challenge I see is the choice to embrace an attitude or mindset that is disempowering**. For some, it's the belief that there are no jobs. For others, it's a debilitating bitterness about a former employment situation. And for still others, it's the belief that they should get their dream job immediately after graduating. These attitudes creep out and make you difficult to employ.

"Avoid the 84th Problem" - There is a story about a troubled individual who climbs a mountain to seek truth from a wise old woman. As he arrives at her hut, the woman greets him, and before he can even speak says, "Ah… I can see you have a problem!"

Shaken, the man asks, "How could you know that?"

The wise woman replies, "Because you have 83 problems."

"How do you know that?" the man asks, somewhat taken back.

The woman sips her green tea and responds, "God has set up the universe to be very fair…everyone has 83 problems."

The man thinks for a minute and then asks, "What am I supposed to do with these problems?"

The woman takes another sip of her tea and says, "Well, some of the problems you solve, some you manage and some you turn into a great opportunity."

"What will happen then?" the man asks.

"Then you'll receive some more problems. Everyone always has 83." The woman adds, "There is only one other problem and that's the 84th."

"What's the 84th problem?" the man asks a little bit irritated.

The old women finishes enthusiastically, "The 84th problem is believing you shouldn't have 83 problems."

I sometimes fall into this disempowering mindset. I start to believe that I shouldn't have problems. This isn't true and it's not helpful. M.

Scott Peck begins *The Road Less Traveled* with these words, "Life is hard." Jesus told us, "In this world you will have trouble."

"Adversity Advantage Mindset" - Work at embracing a more positive approach to problems. The Christian Scriptures teach that all things work together for good, to those that love God and are called to His purpose. Success writer Napoleon Hill taught that, "Every adversity carries with it a seed for benefit." I believe your greatest struggle can become your biggest success as you learn to apply your God-given passion and talent.

"Alchemist Mindset" – Alchemy is turning a substance of lesser value like lead into a substance of greater value like gold. Everyday alchemy is turning a frown into a smile. It's a teacher turning an underachieving student into a kid who works harder than they ever imagined. It's a barista turning an ordinary bean into an uplifting elixir. It's a salesman turning a complaint into a customer for life. It's George Washington Carver turning the peanut into over 300 useful products. And it's you turning unemployment or a job you dislike into the career of your dreams.

There are mindsets, mental models, attitudes and strategic thought processes that work... and that will cause us to find work much faster.

"Abundance Mindset" – Believe and hold the thought that there are many opportunities, even in a down economy. At the height of the last recession, there were still 46 million new hires in 2009. You are not looking for a lot of opportunities. You're only looking for **one** opportunity that allows you to make a big contribution and utilize your unique strengths.

"Add Value Mindset" - This is the attitude of **service and contribution**. Many people go into job search overly focused on what they can get from a job in the way of salary, hours and benefits. It's not that these things aren't important. They just don't come first. It's like saying to a wood burning stove, "Give me some heat... and then I'll put some wood in you." I believe in being a "go-getter". But it's even more important to be a "go-giver".

"Agency Mindset" – Agency is the capacity to exert power and take full responsibility. The agentic perspective believes that people are proactive and self motivated, not just shaped by environment forces. It's very common for job candidates to spend huge amounts of time thinking about, even obsessing, over things they have absolutely no control over. **Successful people focus on things they can do something about.** Unsuccessful people focus on circumstances they have absolutely no control over. That negative focus often results in blaming, complaining and feelings of victimization.

"Appreciation Mindset" – When you're out of work, or working at a job that doesn't fit, it's easy to focus on what's wrong with your life. The problem is, what you focus on expands. It takes up more mind space and it tends to expand in the real world as well. You must discipline yourself to focus on what's working in your life. This is very difficult for me. Sometimes I do an alphabet of gratitude. I usually sing my way through the alphabet and think about something good in my life that begins with each letter. Sometimes I do this with my wife and we trade off on the letters.

"Artist Mindset" – When I say "art", I mean to arrange. Artists arrange musical notes, lines and color on a canvas, ingredients in a food dish, numbers on a spreadsheet, elements in a test tube or ideas in a presentation. We are all artists. This is my go-to mindset. Brainstorming pulls me out of a funk faster than anything.

"Accurate Mindset" – Most of us anticipate the future. A few focus on what could go wrong. Some expect most things to go right. The truth is, we need a plan for multiple scenarios. We need to think about what could go wrong and prepare for it. That's why we buy various kinds of insurance. We also need to plan for wild successes. What if everything went way better than we thought? Many people habitually delude themselves, either positively or negatively, and they pay a price for it. One way I stay connected to "truth" is by spending time in Scripture everyday. These classic thoughts were written over a 1500 year period and they are timeless.

I work on my attitude, strategic thought processes or state of mind and emotions every single day. You will need to as well, if you want to accelerate your job search.

Get Organized

The last part of getting set up for job search is organizational or clerical.

Professional Email – I strongly recommend setting up a *Gmail* account if you don't already have one. An *AOL* account is a strong indicator that you may be older and don't keep up with trends and newer practices. When you are in job search mode, check your email at least 2-3 times per day.

Professional Voicemail – You will benefit from a cell phone and even more from a smart phone. Many job search candidates don't check their voicemail and don't keep their box cleared out so that hiring managers can leave a message. Don't put your home number on your resume and expect that your teenager or toddler will do a professional job of taking messages for you. Like email, voicemail is an important part of the modern job search. A few years ago it was considered acceptable to respond to a message in 24 to 48 hours. In today's world, you should respond in less than 8 hours.

Professional Image and Wardrobe - Don't wait until you get an interview to pick out the clothes. Go shopping now.

Keep Appointments - <u>Always</u> arrive 10 minutes early.

Communicate Positively and Professionally - Never say anything negative about former employers or co-workers. Always be gracious and upbeat.

Conduct Information Interviews - Connect with hiring managers and anyone already working in the type of career you're interested in. If you're not familiar with an informational interview, I recommend the series of books, *PBS Television* series and DVDs put out by *Roadtrip Nation*. You can watch hundreds of informational interviews conducted by students asking questions of successful people in many different types of work.

SUCCESSPATH offers a "Full-Throttle Accelerated Job Search Workshop" that coordinates with the information in this book. And we offer one-to-one support and coaching. Please contact:

Dale Cobb at – dale.successpath@gmail.com

"Most job-hunters who fail to find their dream job fail not because they lack information about the job market, but because they lack information about themselves."

~Richard Bolles

CHAPTER 1
YOUR SIGNATURE STRENGTHS

I define a strength as any resource, internal or external, that helps you make a contribution in the marketplace. Getting crystal clear on your strengths is the first step in an effective job search. Understand your selling points and how you stand out.

Many job search candidates completely misunderstand the purpose of a resume and interview. The purpose is <u>not</u> to share where you've worked. The purpose of a resume and an interview is to effectively describe, display and demonstrate very specific job related strengths which allow you to make a very well-defined contribution in service of a potential employer. Spending a few hours doing some strengths awareness work will help you with the rest of your search including targeting, resume crafting, interview preparation and the job search itself.

Container Store founder, Kip Tindell says:

"1 Great Employee = 3 Good Employees"

Where and how can you become that great employee?

If you are working, someone is paying you to add value or make a contribution. That contribution may include:

Speed, Efficiency, Money, Comfort, Beauty, Control, Experience,

Safety, Quality, Size, Growth, Knowledge, Skill, Freedom, Delivery, Service, Time, Order, Simplicity, Convenience, Confidence, Leisure, Teamwork or Productivity

The contribution may also include the reduction of:

Risk, Problems, Disease, Illness, Limitation, Difficulty, Debt, Boredom, Chaos, Divisiveness, Poverty, Suffering, Hunger, Depression, Racism, Ignorance or Illiteracy

Grab a notebook and write out your thoughts to the following questions. If you don't like writing, have a partner ask you the questions and take notes on your answers.

What gets better when you walk in the room?
What are your contributions?
How do you add value?
Where do positive results show up as a result of your activities?
What is the role or roles where you have been indispensible?
Where are you the Linchpin? Or...
What falls apart when you leave?
What tasks are you invited to perform?
When do people ask you back?
What are your "Encore Activities" where people want a repeat performance?

Adding value is the purpose of your strengths. Like "facets" on a diamond, or lanes on a super highway, each strength will cause you to shine in the workplace or succeed in the marketplace. There are several dozen possible categories and components that comprise your unique set of strengths. Let's look at a few.

Passion

"Do not hire a man who does your work for money, but him who does it for love of it."
~Henry David Thoreau

Passion or enthusiasm is a huge success multiplier. It creates energy and attracts job offers like a magnet. This component might also be referred to as a natural affinity, appetite, strong interest or desire. Your passion is a topic or task you are drawn to. It's an activity or subject area that makes you feel strong.

Richard Bolles said, "Passion plus competency, not just competency alone, is key to securing employment." And Marc Cenedella, founder of *The Ladders* writes, "When two candidates are equally experienced, equally credentialed, and equally capable, who gets the job? The candidate with a passion for the business. A zeal for the industry. An excitement. An enthusiasm. A zest for the art, and the craft, and the science, of what makes a company in the field succeed. And what bosses have discovered is that somebody who is passionate about the business tends to be a better employee and a better professional to work with.

Because somebody who is passionate is inherently motivated, and internally driven to succeed, they try harder to find answers. They think up clever stuff on their own. They enjoy the business, and the customers, and the industry so much that they're always discovering new things or perceiving additional ways that the business could succeed.

In short, passionate people are better employees because they care more than dispassionate people. Passionate people care more than the average employee, they care more than the average applicant, and they care more than you.

And that's why you didn't get the job. It's why you got passed over, turned down, or put in the 'nice to have' pile.

If you truly want success in this business climate, you need to do what you're actually passionate about. Otherwise, you're just unfairly stacking the deck in some other applicant's favor."

I heard Oprah Winfrey share this insight, "Every single person who is super successful always says in some form that following your bliss or **following your passion is the way for you to be the most successful** and empowered person." After forty years of studying human potential, I have to agree.

This does not mean that success is not hard. Steve Jobs told us that it is exactly because success is so very hard that we need to discover our passion. Historically, passion incorporated the idea of suffering. What is it that you love to do so much that you are willing to suffer for it?

I don't believe you will ever maximize your career or become the best version of yourself until you are spending most of your work hours on something that excites you. You can only operate from pure discipline for so long, and then it's exhausting. When you love what you do, you will jump out of bed every morning and will be excited to get to work. And as a result, you will maximize your success. Passion will automatically drive you to work smarter, harder and longer. You will endure failures with comeback after comeback. And that's a great way to spend your time at work.

For some, passion discovery is elusive. Sometimes this is fear, disguised as practicality. Following your passion can be a radical act that must overcome pressure from public opinion, parents, partners, professors and promoters. But the discovery process is worth it. Think about these words of Dr. Wayne Dyer, "There's no scarcity of opportunity to make a living at what you love. There is only a scarcity of resolve to make it happen."

Here are a few inquiries to help you uncover your passions:

Passion Inquiries

What are your intense interests?

Which sections of a bookstore/magazine section pull you?

Where do you spend money after the bills are paid?

What are your regular online stops?

What do you do with your free time?

What's on your calendar?

What do you schedule?

What do you do after work and on weekends?

What gets you going?

What activities give you energy?

What are your "Lights On" subjects? Which topics light you up?

What are your day dreams?

What are you always thinking about?

What's stewing in your mental crock pot?

What music do you listen to?

What are your top 10 favorite songs of all time?

Why do you like them?

What are your favorite lyrics?

What are your favorite movies or TV shows?

What's your "I'd rather be" bumper sticker?

Talent

"Talent hits a target no one else can hit. Genius hits a target no one else can see."
~Arthur Schopenhauer

A critical dimension of a *STRENGTHSPATH Job Search System* is talent. Simply, it's seeking to do what you naturally do best, the way you best do it! Inter-changeable words are inborn ability, potential or gifts. Talent is what you are naturally good at. Spending work time in activities that don't reflect your natural talent is almost always a huge waste of productivity.

There is a myth of "omnicompetence" in both the classroom and the boardroom. You don't have the same potential for success in all arenas. Even recognized geniuses are very limited. Nuclear scientist and *Nobel Prize* Winner Richard Feynman said, "I've learned to draw and read a little bit, but I'm really still a very one-sided person and I don't know a great deal. I have a limited intelligence and I use it in a particular direction." Albert Einstein expressed similar thoughts about talent, "Everybody is a genius. But if you judge a fish by its ability to climb a tree, it will live its whole life believing that it is stupid."

You have a "Talent Triangle" that includes **Aptitudes, Activities** and **Approaches** that drive what you'll be the best at. Consistently seeking and selecting work outside of that triangle is one of the biggest mistakes a job candidate can make .

The first side of our Talent Triangle is **Aptitudes** including:

Words – like communicating, writing and speaking

Numbers – like arithmetic and mathematics

Pictures – like visualizing structures and mechanical objects

Music – like singing or playing an instrument

Body – like coordination and stamina

People – like connecting, befriending and influencing

Self – like awareness and motivation

Nature – like growing plants and raising animals

Existential Thinking - like understanding human purpose

We do not have these aptitudes in the same amounts or combinations. These portions and groupings are part of what make us unique and allow us to add more value in one arena than in another.

Johnson O'Connor began testing for aptitudes in a *General Electric* laboratory in 1922. He soon after formed the *Johnson O'Connor Foundation* that continues to help individuals make better career choices. They are in most of the major U.S. cities and continue to test for aptitudes like:

Graphoria – Managing symbols, **Ideaphoria** – Creating ideas, **Structural Visualization** – Thinking in 3 dimensions, **Abstract Visualization** – Manipulating ideas, **Inductive Reasoning** – Seeing connections in scattered facts, **Analytical Reasoning** – Separating into component parts, **Finger Dexterity** – Moving fingers skillfully, **Tweezer Dexterity** - Handling small tools easily, **Observation** – Taking careful notice, **Design Memory** – Memorizing designs rapidly, **Tonal Memory** – Remembering sounds, **Pitch Discrimination** – Differentiating musical tones, **Rhythmic Ability** – Keeping time, **Timbre Discrimination** – Detecting similar pitch & volume, **Number Memory** – Remembering numbers, **Proportional Appraisal** – Discerning harmonious designs, **Silograms** – Learning languages and technical jargon, **Foresight** – Looking into the future with wisdom, **Color Perception** – Distinguishing colors

The second side of our Talent Triangle is **Activities**. On top of our Aptitudes, we all have Activities that are enjoyable and come very easily to us. We have activities where we are AWESOME, activities where we are AVERAGE and activities where we are AWFUL. Consistently selecting work in activities that are difficult or un-enjoyable isn't wise. In most cases, contrary to popular opinion, trying to get from awful to awesome is a complete waste of time. The effort to get from average to awesome is a poor use of time. Each of us has 3 or 4 activities where we are naturally awesome. Most of our time should be invested in becoming world class at adding value while engaging in those activities.

While there are millions of potential activities and combinations of activities that are potential strengths, our **Activity Talents** will often fall into **Four Types.**

The four include:

- **Activities with People**
- **Activities with Things**
- **Activities with Ideas**
- **Activities with Data/Information**

Think about the four categories above. Is there a little more excitement over one or two categories than the others? Which of the four is your dominant Activity Type? Which is your secondary Activity Type?

Now consider your activities at work. You can focus on current activities if you are employed, but feel free to draw from past ones as well. Get a sheet of paper or open a word processing document and list everything you currently do in the course of a day/week/month/quarter. Use two lines to create three sections or create 3 text boxes. In the first section, write down activities where your performance is somewhere near **Awesome**. In the second section, **Average**. In the third section, write down the activities where your performance is **Awful**. Consider your performance but also include your passion or enjoyment level. Look for patterns of strength and how well your jobs have really fit. About 25-30% of all workers can optimize a role by expanding the position in ways that better engage their strengths. Another 25-30% would be more effective if they trimmed a few activities from their work. One more 25-30% group of workers are altogether miscast for their current role. If this is you... start doing some serious strengths discovery and engage in a full throttle job search.

The third side of our Talent Triangle is **Approaches**. We all have ways of Approaching any activity that work better for us. This is true for any and every role, position or job. In my book, *The STRENGTHSPATH Principle* I talked about the different approaches of stand up comedians, super heroes, U.S. Presidents and later in this book, Supreme Court Justices. In my work as a sales manager and trainer, I noticed very quickly that the best sales reps approached the same job very differently based on their unique mosaic of strengths.

Most of the talent assessments focus on helping individuals better understand their unique approach to a position. Marcus Buckingham's *StandOut* assessment helps workers activate their unique approach to tasks based on 9 roles. These approaches include: **Advisor, Connector, Creator, Equalizer, Influencer, Pioneer, Provider, Stimulator and Teacher.** The assessment focuses on your top 2 or 3 approaches. It will help you understand your sequence of strengths.

Gallup's Strengthsfinder 2.0 assessment helps you understand four approach domains or what I call strength types. These include: **Executing, Influencing, Relationship Building and Strategic Thinking.** Strengthsfinder 2.0 then gets more detailed or more granular. Each of the four domains has underlying strength themes.

Executing Themes include: Achiever, Arranger, Belief, Consistency, Deliberative, Discipline, Focus, Responsibility and Restorative

Influencing Themes include: Activation, Command, Communication, Competition, Maximizer, Self-Assurance, Significance and Woo

Relationship Building Themes include: Adaptability, Developer, Connectedness, Empathy, Harmony, Includer, Individualization, Positivity and Relator

Strategic Thinking Themes include: Analytical, Context, Futuristic, Ideation, Input, Intellection, Learner and Strategic

Both of these assessments are good first steps to better understanding your most natural approach to any current and future job or position.

Talent Inquiries

What are your inborn inclinations?

Identify your "Factory Settings". What did you love doing at ages 5, 6, 7, 8, 9, 10, 11, 12, 13, 14? What were you good at?

What activities and tasks do you have an instinctive feel for?

What's your version of a "green thumb"?

Someone has said we all have about 20,000 moments a day. What are your "Made-For-This-Moments"?

What are the times or activities where you felt like you were made to do that?

What do you find *impossible* not to get involved with?

What can't you not do?

What are you insanely great at?

Where or when are you the most creative?

What are the situations where you come up with ideas?

When do you easily go off script or improvise?

What do you see or notice that other people don't?

In what areas or activities do you grow the fastest?

What are the subjects you learned quickly and easily?

What are the skills you picked up without much effort?

What is your genius?

How are you smart?

Which of your talents aren't getting used?

List the following intelligences in order as you think they show up in your personal hierarchy. Word Smart? Picture Smart? Body Smart? Logic/Math Smart? People Smart? Self Smart? Nature Smart? Existential Smart? Music Smart?

What's inside you trying to get out?

What activities must you do?

Are you better at Execution, Influence, Relationship Building or Strategic Thinking? List them in order.

Personality

"Your personality style is a kind of map of both your inner geography and the outward direction of your life. You follow its path everyday of your life."
~John Oldham M.D. and Lois Morris

Your personality or temperament is a crucial dimension of *STRENGTHSPATH Job Search System*. You must search for work that is harmonious with who you are. Are you an introvert or extravert? Both are great personality styles, but certain roles and positions better fit with one or the other.

People generally behave in patterned, organized and recognizable ways. If we say that someone is outgoing, we usually mean that they are outgoing with some degree of regularity. A pattern is implied. With consistency, we can also say that some traits come packaged together in a unique, yet discernible group that we might call a personality type. Are you more :

Intense or Relaxed?

Shy or Outgoing?

Options Open or Decisive?

Analytical or Active?

Independent or Dependent?

Extraverted or Introverted?

Driven or Carefree?

Cheerful or Serious?

Cautious or Adventurous?

Excitable or Calm?

Leader or Follower?

Friendly or Reserved?

Flexible or Structured?

Detailed or Big Picture?

Sequential or Random?

Quantitative or Qualitative?

Task Oriented or People Oriented?

Fast or Slow?

Each of these traits impact which jobs you will thrive in and which jobs you will dive in. They each impact how **_you_** will work in any role most effectively.

Values

"Make sure your values and the values of the organization are compatible."
~Peter F. Drucker

Your values include your ideals, what's important to you, what you care about, what drives you and what motivates you. If you value a method, a person or object, that means you appreciate and respect them. **Values, when they are aligned, form a group's culture**. Your personal DNA should match the organizational DNA.

If you have a rule, a standard or an ideal, behind it you will find a value. When you use the word "should" there is almost always a value behind it. Families have values. Churches have values. Community service groups have values. Corporations have values. And individuals have values.

All companies have values with regard to things like product quality, speed, beauty, service, customer experience and price point. And in reality they have these values in a sequence, hierarchy or order. No company or customer values them all equally.

In general, your values are a type of strength that will align with the organization and team you are working with. Value conflicts are a huge problem in companies. Value alignment is a huge value.

Financial guru and "get out of debt" advocate Dave Ramsey explains the importance of values this way, "It would be a little tough for me to be passionate about selling credit cards because it goes against my value system."

You want to pursue work that aligns with your personal value system. And you want to pursue work with companies where there is a solid values connection. I've made the mistake of believing I could convince an organization to align with my values. It doesn't happen.

Andy Andrews writes, "The drivers behind your decisions are what will give you the energy to see them through. The more powerful the driver, the more committed you become."

Here are a list of values I often use as a starting point in my Strengths Clarification work using the acrostic M.Y. B.I.G. D.R.I.V.E.R.S.

Mastery - Growth, Development, Progress, Maturity
Yield - Money, Economic, Reward, Return, Compensation

Beauty – Aesthetics, Form, Visual Expression
Influence – Authority, Control, Power

Giving – Service, Altruism, Helping

Discovery – Theory, Knowledge, Understanding, Truth
Regulatory – Structure, Order, Routine, Sameness
Individualistic - Independent, Uniqueness, Autonomy
Variety – Change, Newness, Innovation, Creativity
Excellence – Quality, Craftsmanship, Superiority
Relationships – Co-Workers, Collaboration, Teamwork
Safety – Security, Protection, Guarantees

Ponder these 12 value themes and threads. Attempt to put them in order according to your own hierarchy. Resist sequencing them based on how you think they <u>should</u> be ordered. Then try to do the same with the company where you work. Many top companies have a very heavy focus on hiring people with matching values. This is smart from a hiring perspective. It's really difficult and time consuming to change a person's values. And the same is true for you. Your chances of shifting a company's value set or culture will probably be an exercise in futility and a complete waste of time. Trust me on this. As I mentioned earlier, I've tried.

In her book *Career Comeback*, Lisa Johnson Mandell warns that many job seekers consider values a "luxury item" or in the "nice-to-have" category when it comes to selecting a career or company. But these details can significantly impact your career potential. Are you an indoor person or outdoor person? Are you a smoker? Will your employer make accommodations for that? How important is that exposed tattoo? These issues are all about values.

Learning Style

"Lecture continues to be the most prevalent teaching method in secondary and higher education, despite evidence that it produces the lowest degree of retention for most learners."
~David A. Sousa

The next strengths dimension is your learning style. This is your optimal way of perceiving, organizing, retaining and responding to instruction methods. It's a style or pattern of acquiring and processing information.

The ability to learn quickly is at a premium today. The world of work is changing rapidly. Most experts believe the rate of change is accelerating exponentially. This means that entire professions will be replaced after only a few years existence. To succeed in the coming world you will need to reinvent yourself many times. That means getting crystal clear on your strongest aptitudes, activities and approaches. It means being ever aware of strengths that may have been laying dormant. And it means being aware of your unique learning style.

How do you learn best? Here is a list of seven different approaches to learning. Each category includes a famous person or type of worker that has displayed a strong preference for the style:

Listening? Franklin Roosevelt, Harry Truman, Lyndon Johnson
Reading? Dwight Eisenhower, John Kennedy, Ben Carson
Doing? Builders, Mechanics, Athletes
Writing? Winston Churchill
Talking? Trial Lawyers, Medical Diagnosticians
Drawing or Sketching? Beethoven
Thinking? *Spanx* Founder Sara Blakely

For each of these styles of learning there are **learning gears**. Learn to use the gear shift within each style. Gear one is deep learning. It means a slow breaking down of each piece of information while using one or more of the learning modalities. Gear two happens at a moderate pace. Gear three and above involves summarizing, skimming and scanning. Learn to use all the gears, shifting up and down as the need occurs.

Your learning style is the last of the innate or natural strengths covered in this book. It is the bridge to skills and knowledge which are strengths that must be developed.

Knowledge

"Knowledge and perception are the result of protracted study and reflection."
~Alban Berg

The right knowledge builds your career. Sometimes that means memorizing, sometimes it means muscle memory, sometimes it means knowing where to look and sometimes it means hiring the person who knows where to look. If you always have to look up the same thing everyday, maybe you should invest the time to memorize it. Or maybe you just need to make the knowledge more accessible. Put the information on a 3x5 card or in a binder nearby.

Knowledge often builds synergy with skill as it works on top of the talent/passion foundation. Where skill is about methods, steps and sequences; **knowledge is about awareness and assimilation of principles, rules, information, concepts and facts.** In a strengths context, knowledge can be described as an organized body of information, often of a factual nature and sometimes of a procedural nature. It would be a kind of information that would make performing a certain type of work possible. Work is a combination of knowledge and skill. Some roles are more knowledge oriented.

To excel or become world class, you will need to develop expertise. Work on becoming extremely knowledgeable in the area of your passion, the arena where you'd love to work. **Every profession has a unique language that includes vocabulary, terminology, names for parts, pieces and names for equipment or tools.** If you are a doctor you will need to learn where each body part is located. If you are a lawyer, learning how the law library is organized and where to look for case decisions and legal precedents is critical. If you are a technology specialist you need to learn where the computer components are located and how they fit together. Salespeople benefit from strong product knowledge. One of my favorite examples is the copier salesperson whose basement was full of copiers, including those of the competition. He knew them all inside and out. He could even make minor repairs to the other company machines as a way of adding extra value up front.

Every profession involves pattern recognition, principles, symptoms, and meaning, along with cause and effect relationships. Knowledge allows you to create "distinctions". When I look inside a computer I say, "Yep, it's a computer!" Hopefully, when my repair person at the *Genius Bar* looks, he or she knows with great precision exactly what each piece is and what it does. Distinction leads to accurate diagnostics. These aren't developable skills so much as they are about building an essential knowledge base.

Whatever work you choose, you will need to develop an awareness and a level of understanding of systems, procedures, equipment, theories, rules, laws, codes, precedents and more. In a world of accelerated knowledge and rapid change, life-long learning becomes a high priority. Learning how to learn is paramount!

Skills

"Since the traits and abilities that we measure do not change with training or coaching, would it make sense to know those before we evaluated skills or purchased training to enhance them?"
~Chuck Russell

Skills are what you add to talents in order to transform them into deliverable strengths. A skill is an ability developed through deliberate systematic effort and intentional practice. They are often supported by role models, mentors, training and coaching. Skills include methods, steps, sequences, strategies, tool and technology proficiencies.

Job search is a skill itself which must be developed as you progress in your career. But skill development of all types has the potential to improve your career advancement. Improving your listening skills, clarification skills and presentation skills are all worthwhile investments for people working in most roles. In fact, to engage any work with underdeveloped relevant skill sets is a horrible waste of a career. Are you performing poorly because you are a poor listener? That's terrible career management. Are you performing poorly because you haven't learned to ask good questions? That's terrible career management. Are you failing because you can't communicate or make clear presentations? That's terrible career management.

Whatever you do for a living, there are corresponding realities. Are you a marketer, manager, meat cutter, medical biller or masonry contractor? <u>It doesn't matter what you do, increasing your professional skill level is smart career management!</u> When you build the right skills, you will get a bigger result for the same time and effort.

Spending lots of energy developing the wrong skills is a very common time waster. **Make sure that most of your skill development is matched with your underlying talents.** A skill will grow much faster and make larger contributions when it's based on a natural ability.

Some people spend energy building skills that were really better suited for another season of life. When I see 40 year-olds still spending *20 hours a week* trying to improve their baseball skills, while they struggle at their career, I cringe. This is very appropriate for a 16 year-old, but at 40, not so much.

Skill Inquiries

What is your most developed skill?

Which skill is critical in your current work? Is there a mismatch?

What was the most important skill in your previous job?

If your life depended on naming a skill at which you're in the top 1% of the world, what would it be?

What skill would you enjoy increasing 25% in the next year?

Where are you still trying to grow and get better?

Where do you need to grow?

If there was one thing you'd start doing differently tomorrow to unleash more of your potential, what would it be?

What have you learned how to do? If you had to train or coach someone, what would it be?

Character

"What I call everyday greatness comes from character and contribution."
~Stephen Covey

Character failures undermine success. These failures will undermine the trust you have with clients, partners, peers and supervisors. Consider the following examples:

Most of the U.S. House of Representatives continued to allow themselves insider information privileges on the stock market. A CEO and leaders of a large energy enterprise misrepresented financials, eventually bringing down the entire company and putting thousands out of work. There was the pastor, the parish priest and the football coach. And then there were the brilliant Wall Street bankers whose decisions nearly brought down the United States economy, causing millions to lose jobs.

When I write about character strengths, I mean moral qualities and decisions. In fact, character strengths are the ones we all can choose. Consider the following:

Commitment – Attendance, Punctuality, Follow Up
Hard Work – Industry, Diligence, Action, Initiative
Attitudes – Gratitude, Humility, Humor, Cheer, Fun, Mercy
Respect – Authority, Honor, Politeness, Kindness, Fairness
Attention – Being Fully Present, Anticipation, Awareness
Courage – Boldness, Bravery, Grit
Truth – Sincerity, Scruples, Trustworthiness, Ethics
Excellence – Workmanship, Quality, Presentation, Hygiene
Restraint – Self Control, Discipline, Clean-Sober, Frugality

Why is character so important? Great successes always require collaboration. Collaboration requires trust. And trust only flourishes where character qualities are pervasive. Stephen Covey has said on a number of occasions, that the American literature on "how-to-be-successful" was mostly about character and moral qualities until the early 1900's. At that point, strategy, technique and tactics began to take center stage. Covey also talks about the **Speed of Trust** in his book by that title. Lack of character leads to mistrust. This slows everything down, including entire world economies. Do you want your career to advance faster? Slow down and take the time to build trust in all your relationships!

Experience

"You only lack experience if they want it done the same old way."
~Robert Brault

What type of experience did you get in your last job or first job? Most job search candidates undervalue their early work experiences. Many play down experience in fast food, retail or jobs that demand physical labor. You were exposed to a lot more than you think.

Imagine two job search candidates with identical experience. Each walks into an interview having worked two years at the same *McDonalds*.

The first candidate is asked about their experience and responds:

"I just flipped burgers, that was pretty much it".

Then the second candidate walks in with identical experience but responds:

"My first job was at *McDonalds*. It was the greatest experience of my life. I still have friends that I made while working there. I'm no-where near the person I was when I started. I'm grateful for everything they taught me. I learned how to:

Work with the public
Be responsible
Show up on time
Work under adverse conditions
Handle irate customers
Solve problems and put out fires
Make customers feel comfortable

Work as a team member
Be accountable and work under authority
Implement repeatable systems
Increase my efficiency
Organize, plan and set up
Display ordinary items in an extraordinary way
Process payments
Up-Sell...Do you want fries with that?

The **training was amazing**...It was **great**...It was **wonderful**...I would **do it all over again**..."

The second candidate painted a picture of what they experienced and **how they grew**.

Same experience... who gets the job?

You can learn to understand the strengths in your experiences, and give quality responses!

Many job seekers struggle with the problem of getting experience. It can be a difficult conundrum – companies won't hire you without experience and they won't hire you to get experience.

Sometimes you have to get creative. Much of my experience was gained through volunteer work, either in the community or at churches. I got my earliest coaching experience working in a school program that was called cross-age instruction. I coached softball teams. I took a community volunteer position with *Help In Emotional Trouble,* A Crisis Phone Line where I worked a 4 hour shift once a week for 2 years. I volunteered for *Luis Palau Crusades* and started out as a volunteer stuffing envelopes. The first day on the job they gave me an office key and within a short period of time I was placed on paid staff. I taught classes, workshops and wrote curriculum for free in a church setting.

Eventually I was paid for all these things.

In his book, *Born For This,* Chris Guillebeau tells the story of a personal trainer that wanted to become a yoga instructor. The individual went to the local DVD store and rented every yoga lesson that was available. The next stop was *Amazon* to order a dozen more sets. The budding instructor watched each one, taking detailed notes on terminology and poses.

The following week was "Go Time". The first hour of teaching went well and the new instructor continued three sessions per day, five days per week. The studio is now packed with students and they've actually won awards for the teaching.

Guillebeau reminds us that it's getting easier and easier to self-learn almost anything.

My Dad built a single home with a builder that was a friend of the family. Then Dad went off and started what would become a very successful building business.

Our first client at *Road to Jobs* was Scott Turner. Scott was afraid for his life and trying to get out of a gang. The only thing my Dad could find in his background was that he loved his art classes in school. Dad sat him in front of a *CAD* program designing homes and Scott took to it like a duck to water. Today, he has clients all over the country.

In his book *And More*, Andy Rooney shares a related experience. He writes, "One summer when I was in college, I got a job helping a rigger in a big paper mill. We did heavy odd jobs, and the man I worked with knew how to do everything, it seemed to me. One day our job called for him to run a steam shovel. He just climbed on and went to work with it.

Later, we were sitting on a pile of bricks eating our lunch, and I asked him how he learned to operate a steam shovel. He told me, and what he said was a lesson for young job seekers who say they can't get a job because they have no experience and can't get any experience without a job.

'I read an ad in the newspaper,' he said. 'This guy was looking for someone to run a steam shovel. I got the job and climbed up there and started fooling with the pedals and the hand levers. About an hour later, the boss knew for sure I didn't know what I was doing and got fired. A week later, I got another steam shovel job and I only lasted four days, but by this time I knew a lot about how they worked. The third job I got, I kept because I had all this experience.'"

Rooney finishes, "Somehow that approach to a job appeals to me more than a letter from someone who enumerates his relevant credentials and skills, specific experiences and interests. My suggestion would be that they all learn how to shovel first."

I don't recommend using the following example as an exact model, but it does serve a point. If you haven't seen the movie *Catch Me If You Can* starring Leonardo DiCaprio as Frank Abagnale, check it out. Frank impersonated a *Pan American* airline pilot and flew all over the world. For 11 months, Abagnale impersonated a chief resident pediatrician in a Georgia hospital under the alias Frank Williams. He passed the Louisiana bar exam without a law degree, and got a job at the *Louisiana State Attorney General's* office at the age of nineteen. Frank eventually went to jail for this and more.

Keep it safe and legal but you can get creative!!!

School

In his crazy-wonderful book, *Secrets of a Buccaneer-Scholar,* James Marcus Bach talks about "Schoolism" – the belief that schooling is the necessary and exclusive way to get a good education. Bach describes "Education" as the "you" that emerges from the learning you do.

Clearly, education can happen in or out of school. That being said, school, including diplomas, report cards, grade point averages, degrees, certificates or certifications, can be a strength. Even a record of some coursework can be a positive.

Tools

Certainly tools are external resources that can be turned into marketplace contributions. At a basic level, this might include appropriate work clothes and transportation to and from work. It could be comprised of a work truck with very specific tools, a laptop computer or a computer repair kit. In my case, it includes my *MacBook Pro* and my Career Development Library. Whatever work you do, I recommend building a great set of tools.

Tool Inquiries

What is your "Alchemical Object", something like a wand that allows you to work magic? For Harold, in the children's book by Crockett Johnson, it was his Purple Crayon. For Picasso, it was a paint brush. For Jimi Hendrix, it was his guitar that he reportedly slept with. For Dr. Ben Carson, it was a scalpel. For Stephen Curry, it's a basketball behind the 3-Point line.

What tools do you currently own?

Which tools would optimize your performance?

Are there tools that would increase your chance of getting hired?

"Write down a goal that sends a genuine thrill through your body!"

~Sam Bennett

CHAPTER 2
YOUR SIGNATURE TARGETS

"Where are you on the path towards what you really want?"
~Oprah Winfrey

This section is about setting up authentic career goals, targets, outcomes or destinations.

An effective job search connects your strengths to your career goals. Your targets or goals must flow from your strengths. You must pick, plan and pursue goals that are connected to your natural passion, potential and personality. Most people who struggle in a career, have established targets that are disconnected from their strengths. They are aiming at goals that are not authentic. The talent-target disconnect is the biggest reason most people fail to build successful careers.

How Most Of Us Select Careers

Programs – The television or movie image of a career may be very different than the real day-to-day tasks. I grew up watching *Perry Mason*, a televised version of criminal trial lawyers. I never saw Perry crack a law book or do any research, a big part of real lawyer work.

My first career goal was "Cowboy" based on my hero Roy Rogers, King of the Cowboys. I had the guns, the dog, the hat, and most of all the boots. My first effort at job shadowing was a ride along at the local stables. But I quickly found that horses would look back at me with distinct expressions of disgust. When I discovered that "real" cowboying often involved camping, that was enough for me. The realization 40 years later that that career choice would have been completely devoid of my daily trip to Starbucks solidly confirmed the wisdom of my decision.

Looking back, that was really my first big career insight. I liked the idea of "being" a cowboy, but I didn't much care for the real world daily activities. The "doing" of cowboy activities didn't fit with who I was. I had fallen in love with what my grandmother called a "drug store" cowboy. This fictionalized version was so named because it was common at that time to film the actor sitting on top of a drugstore soda fountain stool instead of a horse.

This is a common error young people make. They fall in love with a romanticized version of a job often portrayed on television. Unfortunately, that scripted version has very little to do with the day-to-day reality of the job.

Programs on television are only one example of a popular but poor way to select a career. Linda Gale, leader of the *National Career Aptitude System*, says that, *"Five out of six people find themselves in a job by accident."*

Practicality – Entrepreneurship blogger Evan Carmichael observes, "Most people chose their path out of fear disguised as practicality." Think about that one for a minute... Does it have a ring of truth for you?

Other faulty ways of selecting a career include:

Postings - Some people just apply for whatever career is posted on an internet job board or career site without much thought. Newspaper classified ads aren't as popular as they once were, but people still select a job this way.

Plant Hiring - Somebody informs you that this or that company is hiring and you head over to the hiring office.

Peer Pressure - Your friend is working for a particular employer and you enjoy spending time together. They tell you about an opening and off you go for an interview.

Partner Pressure – Sometimes a significant other can bring pressure to do some kind of work that is not aligned with your unique design.

Promoters – Be wary of salespeople. This includes the latest infomercial and the admissions representatives at the local college whether it is private, public or profit based. Warren Buffett says, "Never ask a barber if you need a haircut." I've been in selling, sales management and sales training all of my life. There are exceptional sales people who will tell you when you don't need a product or when another product might serve you better. But they are still rare.

Peter Principle Promotions – The Peter Principle says, "Employees get promoted up the ladder until they get promoted into a role that doesn't fit them." Great sales people are promoted into management roles where they don't have the same innate ability. Engineers get promoted into roles where they lack the necessary natural talent to work well with people. This even happens with initial hiring. Great students in the architecture program do not always turn into great architects. This is why *Apple* generally hires people into roles where they are expected to work forever. They may move up dramatically in compensation as they get better at their job, but they are rarely allowed to change positions and move up a corporate ladder. *New York Life Insurance* recognized this as have many great sales organizations. Top sales people often earn much more than managers and are encouraged to make a career of it. Mediocre sales people are often re-directed into the management program. This is almost always true with great coaches in sports. The top coaches were rarely, if ever, great players. All of the great coaches were mediocre players who had a great talent for coaching.

Professors – School teachers at all levels and even career counselors have been occasionally known to offer horrifically discouraging career advice. Jack Canfield tells the story of Horse Whisperer Monty Roberts. When Monty was in high school, his teacher gave the class an assignment to write about what they wanted to be when they grew up. Monty wrote that he wanted to own a 200-acre ranch and raise Thoroughbred racehorses. His teacher gave him an F and explained that the grade reflected an unrealistic dream. No boy who was living in a camper on the back of a pickup truck would ever be able to amass enough money to buy a ranch, purchase breeding stock, and pay the necessary salaries for ranch hands. When he offered Monty the chance of rewriting his paper for a higher grade, Monty told him, "You keep the F; I'm keeping my dream."

Susy and I have visited Monty's 154-acre *Flag Is Up Farms* in Solvang, California. Monty raises Thoroughbred racehorses and trains hundreds of horse trainers in a more humane way to "join-up" and train horses.

Professional Propaganda – Professional advice makes so much sense and it often comes backed with statistics … but it is as dangerous as the others. So many seeking a career look at the latest statistics to discover career trends. Some of the information is old and irrelevant. Jessica Dilullo Herrin is the founder of *Stella & Dot Family Brands*. In her book, *Find Your Extraordinary,* Jessica shares an experience with the guidance counselor at *Glendale Community College* where she attended. The counselor told her she was wasting her time applying to *Stanford* even though she was earning straight A's. The counselor actually laughed in her face. Jessica was admitted to *Stanford* and graduated in 1994.

Sometimes it's just faulty professional opinions. Oprah was told she would never make it in television. Harrison Ford was told he didn't have what it took to make it as an actor.

Polls and Percentages - Some statistics may be intentionally skewed by those in the corporate world who will benefit from too many graduates in a particular field. This allows them to hire at rock bottom wages. Andrew Hacker holds degrees from *Amherst College*, *Oxford College* and *Princeton University*. He is currently a professor emeritus in Political Science at *Queens College*. He explains this in his book, *The Math Myth: And Other Stem Delusions*. Hacker writes, "We've always known businesses like an oversupply of workers, in part to keep those with jobs fearing that they'll be replaced. And, of course, the less money that has to go to the rank-and-file, the more there will be to distribute among the executive suites." Hacker suggests that, "The shortage mantra is all about industry wanting to lower wages."

Remember this next time you hear there is a huge number of openings for this career or that job. This is one reason I tell my clients, "Forget about the hot jobs. Get in touch with what burns inside of you!" Horseshoeing is no longer a profession with a lot of job openings. But if you have the passion and the talent, that's what you should pursue. There are regions of the country where you can make a very good living at this if you're really good.

The other focus of Hacker's book is to debunk the current over focus on Science, Technology, Engineering and Mathematics or STEM. He makes a strong case that only 5% of us will work in jobs that require more than basic arithmetic and a little algebra. Hacker shows that the recent higher math requirements account for a large percentage of both high school dropouts and failure to complete college. He cites research suggesting that most of the current math teachers have absolutely no idea of how their coursework applies in the real world.

Parental Pressure - I didn't receive any pressure from my parents to pursue a particular career. But I'm still convinced it's a very big issue so I'm going to expand on this one.

Mamas, Don't Let Your Babies Grow Up To Be Cowboys is a Country Western tune popularized by Willie Nelson. The chorus of the song features the title line and continues, "make them be doctors and lawyers and such". If you're a parent getting advice from song lyrics or are otherwise predisposed to push or pull a child toward one career or another, please think about this.

Former *General Electric* CEO Jack Welch and his wife Suzy tell a story in their book *Winning,* that represents this trap very well. A student was about to graduate from *Harvard* and he set up an appointment to get career advice from one of Jack's friends, a woman who was very familiar with investment banking and management consulting. The woman said she answered each question the young man had very thoroughly, and he took good notes. But he wasn't especially curious about anything. After 30 minutes, he thanked her politely and stood up to leave. As he did this, he stuck his note pad inside a folder and she noticed that it was totally covered with very detailed drawings of cars.

"Wow, those are amazing! Who did them?" she asked.

In the blink of an eye the student was full of energy as he said, "I did—I'm always drawing cars... my dorm room is covered with posters and paintings of cars—I subscribe to every car magazine! I've been obsessed with cars since I was five years old. My whole life, I've wanted to be a car designer. That's why I'm always going to car shows and *NASCAR* races. I went to Indianapolis last year—I drove there!"

Jack's friend tried to convince the student that he actually belonged in Detroit or working for a car company. But he deflated just as quickly as he had come to life a few minutes earlier, "My dad says the car business is not what I went to *Harvard* for."

She wasn't surprised when she bumped into the father a few months later and he proudly told her that his son was working 80 hour weeks at a *Wall Street* firm.

Jack Welch continues, "I know someone who literally became a doctor because his entire childhood, his mother—a Polish immigrant who loved the American Dream—introduced him by saying, 'And here's my doctor!' He didn't hate the profession, but you've never met anyone more eager to retire."

Welch summarizes his thoughts with this: "**Working to fulfill someone else's needs or dreams almost always catches up to you.**"

Isaac Newton followed his inner pull and became a world class physicist, mathematician, astronomer, and theologian. Imagine if he had followed his mother's desire that he run the family farm. Dvorak and Handel were world class composers. Dvorak's father wanted him to become a butcher and Handel's father hoped that he would pursue law.

John Mackey shared his decision to start *Whole Foods* in an interview with Oprah Winfrey. His mother pleaded with John to go back to school and become a doctor or lawyer. She was convinced he was wasting his life as a grocer.

If you are a parent, your role should be one of objectively trying your best to help your child discover their own unique design, passions, talents and then support them relentlessly in their pursuit. If you are a child of a pushy parent, adult or otherwise, it's critical that you respectfully listen to their viewpoint and then go on to run your own race. Get busy following your *STRENGTHSPATH*, the trail of gifts and desires God has placed deep inside of you.

I love the *Amplified Bible's* Translation of Proverbs 22:6, "Train up a child in the way he should go [**and in keeping with his individual gift or bent**], and when he is old he will not depart from it."

There are probably a variety of reasons parents push their kids toward work that is often unsuited for them. Some parents want to continue building their own business and legacy. Some parents are trying to live their lives vicariously through their children. Fathers are particularly guilty of these two. If I had a son, I'm sure I would have nudged him pretty hard toward baseball, hoping he could do what I didn't. For some parents it may be pride, for others, security. Mothers may be particularly inclined to push their kids in the direction of jobs that they feel are "secure". This may be especially true if a father didn't provide what they considered a level of financial security.

Goal achievement is the most natural thing in the world. We are **teleological beings** who are directed toward an end and shaped for purpose.

Do you struggle with setting goals?

Do you hate setting goals?

Do you fail to reach many or most of the goals you set?

For most of us, the reason is that our goals are not strengths-based...

Our Gifts have been severed from our Goals.

Our Aims are not Authentic.

Our Targets have been disconnected from our Talents.

Our Purpose has been detached from our Passion.

Our Vision has no connection to our Values.

In the middle of every bulls-eye, should be a *heart* to represent your passion and a *star* to represent your natural talents. Direction, especially career direction, should be well informed by a solid understanding of your natural and developed strengths.

Tony Robbins says, "People are not lazy. They simply have impotent goals – that is, goals that do not inspire them." This is true. Many people set goals that are not authentic. They also use processes and frameworks that don't suit them. One size doesn't fit all when it comes to setting up strong targets.

Target Exercises

Grab a notebook and work through the following questions and prompts:

Imagine - Imagine waking up tomorrow morning, and everything about your job is changing. Your work is shifting to something amazing. What exactly are you seeing, hearing and feeling? **Most importantly, what are you doing?** How are you doing it? Where are you doing it? Who are you collaborating with? How do you recognize that this is in fact your dream job?

Describe you Ideal Work Day/Week/Month - Grab 7 sheets of paper representing the days of the week. Write down 8 to 12 hours of productive activities doing exactly what you want. The activities can be anything as long as they make a contribution to someone else's life. My ideal day/week/month is fairly evenly divided among 4 activities – Research, Writing, Coaching 1-to-1, and Training Groups on how to build a successful career that serves others.

Describe Your Dream Job

Using your strengths as a foundation and your Ideal Day/Week/Month as a clarifier, write a paragraph or a page describing your dream job on the next page. Focus on the tasks that are passion and talent based. Make most of your description about what you want to do on a daily basis.

Passion: What will you be excited about?

Purpose: What will you accomplish?

Potential: What talents and aptitudes will you enjoy using?

Process: What are the tasks and activities you will be performing with excellence?

Problems: What kind of problems will you solve?

People: What kind of people will you be working with?

Progress: How will you learn, grow and develop?

Place: What will your work environment be like?

Pay: What will you be earning per year?

Create A Contribution Statement

Write your contribution statement beginning with the word "Because". Follow it with a summary of the problem you will solve or solution you will provide.

Contribution Statement Example:

Because less than 20% of workers use their strengths everyday, I will train and coach individuals how to discover, develop and deliver their unique strengths in the marketplace.

Create a Professional Objective Statement

Include:
• Role and responsibilities
• Functional tasks you will perform
• Ultimate direction and progression

Create a Target Market Statement

Include:
• Geographic flexibility
• Industries you want to pursue
• Preferred size, style and culture of an organization

Create a 100 Targets List

If there are limited opportunities to pursue your dream job in the company where you work, you will need to look at other organizations. *Google Maps* is an excellent way to develop your Target List. Go to https://maps.google.com. Type in the category of employer that hires people to do the kind of work you're interested in. Include the zip code. Example: doctors 93210

A-B-C-D Steps

Sometimes it can be helpful to think in steps. **No one gets their dream job in a single magical maneuver.** Five to seven years of consistent, diligent effort is about average for a career transition requiring extensive education or training. But with a little planning, you get into your chosen arena fairly quickly.

Step A: Any Job_____ This can be a temporary "Assignment". Get in the arena where you want to work doing something similar. This used to be called, "Starting in the mail room". If you don't know what you want to do, take Steve Jobs' advice and get a job washing dishes.

Step B: Better Job_____ Shape the job so it fits better or make a strategic move closer to your dream. Sometimes a better job is a lateral move with regard to pay. In some cases a better job will initially mean a reduction in pay.

Step C: Career _____ You're getting close to the dream doing many tasks you love and are good at.

Step D: Dream Job_____ 80% of your job involves topics and tasks you love. You're using your talents everyday. This is your calling. It's what God put you on the planet to create.

Target the Arena

Writer James Altucher has worked with *HBO, Miramax, Universal, BMG* and *Sony* and has some background with film and television. He shares the story about his *Uber* driver who came to Los Angeles because he wanted to write films but wasn't getting any work. James suggested trying television since only a few films are made each year. TV offers multiple new opportunities with *Netflix, Amazon, Hulu, Apple,* as well as established cable and the older broadcast networks.

The *Uber* driver said he even had a contact inside one of the television shows that would give him immediate work. But he said, "My heart is in cinema… I will only do cinema."

Altucher has a DJ friend who will only play her own music. She makes almost no money and has to support herself working a retail job. She won't do weddings or bars to get established and get her name out there.

This was a constant theme in my work as a career services coordinator. Students would get a certificate or degree in medical billing and refuse to take a foot in the door job at a medical office. They were unwilling to get a medical receptionist job and then make the easy segue to billing.

To get started, target any job in the arena where your dream job resides. It's much easier to go from television writer to film writer than it is to go from *Uber* driver to film writer. As Altucher says, "It's all about learning the art of the transition."

Target Clarity

Most people select career targets before they are clear on what people in a profession actually do on a day-to-day basis. *O*NET* is a resource that provides a reasonably accurate list of professional tasks for over 800 professions. To use this resource, go to www.onetonline.org . In the *Occupation Quick Search*, in the upper right hand corner, type in the name of your target job or profession. You will come to a page of positions that are loosely in your field. Click on the one that is most similar to your career target. This will bring you to a page that displays a sample of reported job titles. I just typed in *Accounting* and came up with 14 professional occupations that are related to this field. Click on any of the 14 occupations and you will be directed to a detailed "Summary Report" on that specific job. A few lines down you'll find "Tasks" with a + symbol. Click on the + and it will expand the tasks. **Here is a modified task list similar to what you might find for accountant:**

- Operate accounting software to record and analyze information
- Check financial documents for correct entry, accuracy and codes
- Classify, record, and summarize numerical and financial data
- Compile and keep financial records
- Enter debit, credit, and total accounts on spreadsheets and databases
- Operate 10-key to produce calculations and documents
- Receive, record, and bank cash, checks, and vouchers
- Comply with federal, state, and company regulations
- Compile financial, accounting or auditing reports and tables
- Record receipts, expenditures, payables, receivables, profit/loss
- Code records according to company procedures
- Reconcile and report discrepancies found in documents
- Access financial information to answer questions
- Match order forms with invoices, and record necessary information
- Perform personal bookkeeping services
- Prepare deposits, verify and balance receipts, sending payments
- Prepare trial balances
- Calculate, prepare, and issue bills, invoices and statements
- Calculate and prepare payments
- Compute deductions for income and social security taxes
- Prepare and process payroll information
- Reconcile printouts and manual journals
- Reconcile bank transactions
- Transfer journal details to general ledger or data sheets
- Complete and submit tax forms and returns
- Prepare workers' comp forms, pension forms, documents
- Prepare purchase orders and expense reports
- Monitor status of loans ensuring payments are up to date
- Calculate amounts due, interest, balances, discounts

- Calculate equity and principal
- Calculate material cost, overhead, expenses, estimates, pricing
- Prepare budget from estimated revenue, expenses and prior budget
- Maintain inventory records
- File, answer phones, handling correspondence

As you read through the list, imagine yourself doing these tasks on a daily basis. If, based on your strengths from the last chapter, you are a good fit for accounting, you might get a burst of energy as you read it. If, like me, you dropped out of accounting in high school and have had a long standing love-hate relationship with excel spreadsheets, you may feel a cold shiver go up your spine. Even thinking about a job in accounting is scarier than a Stephen King novel. If that's you, cross accounting off your list.

Job Shadows

If you get the burst of energy, double check it. Try to set up a job shadow with an accountant friend of the family or walk into an accountant's office, introduce yourself and ask for permission to spend some time observing someone doing the actual work.

Volunteer Work

If the work still excites you, try to get some experience volunteering as a bookkeeper.

Job Zones

Most professional categories have 5 different job zones with ascending levels of education and preparation requirements. By starting out working in the lower zones, you can quickly begin working in the career arena you have the passion and talent for and… you can get paid for exposure to the higher zones. Here are the job zones arranged by the *Department of Labor* and found on *O*NET*.

A job zone is a group of occupations that are similar in:

Education and formal training needed to do the work

Related experience needed to do the work

On-the-job training needed to do the work

Pay is usually higher with the upper zones

Zone 5: Involves Extensive Preparation - May Require a Master's Degree or Doctorate with Extensive Experience

Zone 4: Involves Considerable Preparation - Often Requires a Bachelor's Degree and Several Years Specific Related Experience

Zone 3: Involves Medium Preparation - Requires Vocational School, Some College and Sometimes One or Two Years Experience

Zone 2: Involves Some Preparation - Requires HS Diploma, Few Months to One Year Experience is Common

Zone 1: Involves Little or No Preparation - May Require HS Diploma, GED, Few Days to Few Months of Training, Often On-The-Job

The accounting arena might look something like this:

Zone 5: Chief Financial Officer
Zone 5: CPA
Zone 4: Accountant
Zone 4: Auditor
Zone 4: Financial Planner
Zone 3: Bookkeeper
Zone 3: Payroll Clerk
Zone 3: Credit Counselor
Zone 2: Tax Preparer
Zone 1: Bill Collector
Zone 1: Bank Teller

The medical arena looks something like this:

Zone 5: Surgeon
Zone 5: Doctor of Internal Medicine
Zone 5: General Practice
Zone 5: Medical Intern
Zone 4: LPN - Nurse Practitioner
Zone 4: RN - Registered Nurse
Zone 3: LVN – Licensed Vocational Nurse
Zone 3: EMT - Emergency Medical Technician
Zone 3: Medical Scribe
Zone 2: Medical Biller
Zone 2: Medical Secretary
Zone 2: Medical Receptionist
Zone 2: Phlebotomist
Zone 1: Candy Striper Volunteer

The education arena looks something like this:

Zone 5: Graduate School Professor
Zone 5: University Professor
Zone 4-5: Adjunct Professor
Zone 4-5: Community College Professor
Zone 4: High School Teacher
Zone 4: Elementary Teacher
Zone 3: Substitute Teacher
Zone 3: Classified Instructor
Zone 2: Paid Tutor
Zone 1: Volunteer Literacy Tutor

Every career won't have an elaborate sequence of steps like these three professions but most will have something similar. **There are also ways to advance in income without going up the hierarchy**. For example, if you really love the work as an Emergency Medical Technician, you could decide to go to medical school. But you could also start an ambulance company. If you really enjoyed tutoring, you could become a teacher. But you could also start a tutoring company. In Asia, top tutors are like rock stars in America. They can earn millions of dollars per year.

Marty's Story

When targeting the right career, nothing takes the place of personal exposure and experimentation in the arena.

Marty is a family member who is considering medical school. He's smart, has the grades and the 4 year degree in a science to move forward. But Marty has wisely conducted a couple of job experiments. After college, he went to Emergency Medical Training (EMT) School and worked briefly on an ambulance team. Still interested, he moved on to experiment number two. He took further coursework in medical terminology and got a job at a top hospital working as a scribe. This gives him the opportunity to observe many specialties and further dial in his career choice while getting paid. Marty is brilliant!!!

The 100 Job Exercise

The last suggestion I have for career selection or targeting is the *100 Jobs Exercise* designed by *Harvard Business School* Career Development Director Timothy Butler. He describes the exercise thoroughly in his book *Getting Unstuck*. As the title suggests, the tool is great for people who are struggling to identify a career choice. If you've already made a choice, this exercise should be confirming and possibly help you dial in your choice even tighter. Although I introduce it here in the *Target* chapter, the *100 Jobs Exercise* can also shed additional light on the strengths we talked about in the last chapter.

I've taken Butler's concept and modified it to dovetail with the *ONET* System. The synchronization with *ONET* will allow you to do fairly deep research into the actual day-to-day tasks. Beyond that, the *100 Jobs Exercise* tool is also a way to elicit deep images and aspects of yourself that are not being currently expressed sufficiently in your current life or work situation. In other words, it's a way to identify passion, talents and values that aren't being expressed. It's also a useful tool to identify what Butler calls "Dynamic Tensions". If for example, you select Military

Officer, Homemaker and Surgeon in this exercise, you have some dynamic tensions that will need to be integrated. There are any number of dynamic tensions that can occur. Maybe you have both a desire to "manage people" and you also have a desire to "make strong individual contributions". Or you could have a desire to "work alone" and a desire to "be the one in charge".

100 Job Exercise Directions

Read through the list of 100 job titles on the following page. Circle or place a √ next to 10 roles that you instinctively feel would be enjoyable, energizing or exciting work. Move quickly through the list and use your intuitive first impression. **Do Not** consider whether or not you have the required knowledge or skills to perform well. **Do Not** consider financial rewards. Just identify 10 workplace roles that you feel might be the most enjoyable or exciting.

Accountant	Financial Analyst	Political Science Professor
Admin Services Manager	Fine Artist (Paint, Sculpt)	Police Officer
Advertising Copywriter	Firefighter	Post Office Service Clerk
Advertising Sales Agent	Food Service Manager	Professional Athlete
Arbitrator-Mediator	Foreign Language Translator	Program Director Radio/TV
Architect	Fundraiser	Proofreader
Automobile Mechanic	Graphic Designer	Public Relations Specialist
Bank Branch Manager	High School Teacher	Quality Control Analyst
Bookkeeper	Home Economics Teacher	Real Estate Salesperson
Broadcast News Analyst	Homemaker	Registered Nurse
Carpenter	Human Resources Manager	Research Scientist
Chief Executive	Industrial Production Mgr	Retail Salesperson
Child-Care Worker	Investigative Reporter	Retail Store Manager
City Planner	Investment Fund Manager	Secretary Admin. Assistant
Civil Engineer	Legislator	Senior Military Leader
Computer System Manager	Librarian	Set Exhibit Designer
Computer Systems Analyst	Lodging and Hotel Manager	Ship Captain
Computer User Support	Logistical Planner	Social Service Manager
Counseling Psychologist	Management Analyst	Social Worker
Courtroom Lawyer	Manufacturing Engineer	Sociologist
Creative Writer	Marketing Manager	Software Designer
Credit Counselor	Marketing Researcher	Solar Thermal Tech Installer
Data Entry	Mathematician	Speech Pathologist
Director Religious Activities	Medical Health Service Mgr	Sports Coach
Director, Stage, Film, TV	Medical Scientist	Sports Official
Economist	Meeting Event Planner	Statistician
Education Administrator	Military Serviceperson	Stockbroker Securities Sales
Education Teacher	Museum Conservator	Surgeon
Electrical Engineer	Music Composer Arranger	Technical Product Sales
Electrician	Newspaper Editor	Theoretical Physicist
Emergency Medical Tech	Operations Manager	Treasurer Controller
Entertainer (Actor, Singer)	Optometrist	Veterinarian
Farm and Ranch Manager	Personal Financial Advisor	Video Game Designer
File Clerk	Philosophy Teacher	

100 Job Exercise Directions (part two)

After you've selected your top ten, write them down on a sheet of paper or in the space provided below. If any of the ten choices are equal, you can note that by having multiples of any number. For example, if two choices were a tie for number one, place number one next to both choices.

100 Job – Top 10 List

1.

2.

3.

4.

5.

6.

7.

8.

9.

10.

Inquiries & Insights

Identify any similar jobs or connecting themes between the roles you selected. Theme possibilities include: Action, Analysis, Autonomy, Creativity, Contact, Control, Energy, Entrepreneurship, Finance, Helping People, In The Spotlight, Individual Contribution, Influence, Intellectual Challenge, Interpersonal Communication, Love of Technology, Managing, Power, Problem Solving, Service, Structure, Tangible Products, Teamwork. You may come up with other themes on your own.

Identify any dynamic tensions or incompatibilities between the roles you selected. Dynamic tension possibilities include: Individual Contribution & Teamwork, Action & Analysis, Variety & Sameness, Risk & Safety.

Identify any spontaneous images or songs that came up during the exercise. Maybe an image of a real or fictional person performing a particular task flashed in your mind. This is important because it may suggest the primary activities you believe the role involves. (This may or may not be distorted.) That activity may also suggest another set of work roles where that activity is at the core. Songs are more symbolic but could still provide useful information.

Insights To Implementation

List the jobs or careers you will target for exploration in the first column on the grid below. Include any jobs that came to mind even though they weren't on the 100 list.

List anyone you know that works in that field or is connected to someone working there. Do a *LinkedIn* search to add to your list and study the education and work histories of those profiles.

List key questions that you would like answered from people working in those roles.

Log onto the *ONET* website (https://www.onetonline.org) and find the **Occupation Quick Search** in the upper right corner. Type in a job title you circled from the exercise and hit the return or enter key. One or more career matches should come up on the screen. Click on the match closest to your career interest. A summary report will come up for that occupation. Study the Tasks, Technology Skills, Tools Used, Knowledge, Skills, Abilities, Work Activities, Detailed Work Activities, Work Context, Job Zone, Education, Credentials, Interests, Work Styles, Work Values and Related Occupations. By using the + sign next to each of these categories you can expand the list to include more information.

Create an action plan to contact people you know and connect with a few people through *LinkedIn* mail.

Jobs/Careers	Contacts	Questions

DREAM JOB!!!

"Your resume is the most financially important document you'll ever own. When it works, the doors of opportunity open for you. When it doesn't work, they won't."

~Martin Yate

Chapter 3
Your Signature Resume Package

The purpose of your resume is to clearly communicate your strengths and how they can make a contribution to the organization in the specific role you are a candidate for.

Your resume is a marketing piece designed to show how you will add value. Always make sure your resume presents the **best version** of you. A well written resume should get you the interview. Beyond that, in the case of a close competition, it could become a tie-breaker.

A complete resume package will include several pieces if you want to **stand out** from other candidates and increase your chances of getting hired. The pieces may include:

- Master resume
- Targeted resume customized to a specific position
- Master cover letter
- Targeted cover letter customized to a specific position
- Reference sheet with contact information
- Endorsement sheet with brief comments on your work
- Reference letters from co-workers, customers and employers
- Interview leave behind
- Portfolio which may include all of the above plus target position description, certificates, school transcripts and work samples

First craft a strong master resume. From that master, create customized targeted resumes for each specific job opening. In a sense, every resume you deliver should be a unique one-of-a-kind document!

A good resume should be easy to read for both man and machine (computers). And remember the 10-second rule. That's all most hiring managers will spend reading your marketing tool. You have to communicate a lot in a little space.

Having a modern employer friendly resume is a critical job search component that will help you land interviews and ultimately job offers. Today's resume needs to be **formatted so that it will pass through over 200 different Applicant Tracking Software** programs**. And they must be targeted or customized for each individual opening. The generic resume is a thing of the past.** Here's a general guide on how to write a good resume that will get you more interviews.

Resume File Name

This may seem like a trivial detail, but it's not. NEVER send your resume in with "Resume" as the file name. Imagine you're the hiring manager or HR Director receiving hundreds of resumes for a posted position. Their inbox is flooded with attachments that are all named "Resume". If you want your resume to stand out in a positive way, always place your name in the file. If it's not too long, you might also include the name of position you are applying for. Sometimes companies post different positions all at once. This will make it easier for the person responsible for sorting them.

Word Version

There is some controversy among job search professionals about the preferred method of sending a digital version of your resume. I strongly recommend that you save and send your resume in *Microsoft Word 1997-2003*. Some offices still use older versions of software. Never use *DOCX*. Older Applicant Tracking Software does not always read PDF files. A PDF is preferred if the employer requests it, if Applicant Tracking

Software is not being used or if you know for sure that the software is fairly new.

Resume Format or Type

There are four main types of resume formats: chronological, functional/skills, combination and creative.

The **chronological resume** focuses on work experience in reverse chronological order, most recent experience first. The problem with the pure chronological resume is that it doesn't do a good job calling attention to your strengths and contributions. This format is also a problem if you don't have much experience in the field you are trying to enter.

The **functional/skills resume** focuses on your relevant professional skills. Most hiring managers like to see work history so I don't recommend a pure functional resume either.

The **combination resume** is the best of both worlds. It allows you to begin the resume focusing on your relevant skills and how you can add value. Then you continue with selections of your work history written in a way that highlights transferable skills and experience. I generally recommend that you conclude the resume with education. Although if you have no work experience, you might move the education section up closer to the top of the page.

The **creative resume** is recommended for creative professions like Web Design and 3D Animation. If you can do a good job with it, you might also choose this style for less creative professions. But be careful. They don't work well with Applicant Tracking Software. They may detract from the content and if the company or industry is very conservative, it may be a turn-off.

Regardless of whether you'll be focusing your resume on your work experience or your education and training, there is a simple structure for resumes that you can follow. Here are the various sections that are usually included in a resume. Let's walk through a resume sample. I will use an accounting or financial services position as an example to give you an idea of content for one type of job.

Resume Header

This section includes basic contact information: your name, address, phone number, and email address. If you have a personal website or LinkedIn profile, you can include their URLs. **Don't use the 'header' function on Microsoft Word or other word processors**, because the Applicant Tracking Software programs often fail to recognize them. So despite the fact that the header function might give it a nice looking design, you risk having the software put your resume in the discard pile. Always avoid using text boxes of any kind for the same reason.

Header Example:

FIRST LAST

City, ST Zip | 805.555.5555 | firstlast@gmail.com | LinkedIn

Resume Customized Target

I recommend using the specific name of the position as it's posted or named in the position description. Don't go generic here and assume the hiring manager will know that the *Book Keeping Support* at the top of your resume means the same as *Accountant* at the top of their position description. The company may have multiple positions posted in the accounting department.

Customized Target Example:

Capital Management Specialist

Accounting | Statistics | Business Management | Compliance

Resume Value Statement

In the past, resumes commonly started with an introductory block of text in the form of an objective statement. This usually included what kind of job you were looking for and what you wanted out of it.

I strongly recommend that you drop the objective statement that has been used at the top of a resume for decades. They focus on what the candidate wants instead of what the employer wants. This is a bad strategy. Instead, use a value statement often called a summary or profile. To be candid, most employers are focused on quickly identifying what you have to offer them. The faster you can get there, the better. Offer a quick rundown of your strengths and how you can contribute. You might include your relevant experience, education, expertise and areas of excellence. If you have one or two achievements that can be communicated **using numbers or percentages**, that's even better. This section should be customized using a few keywords from the position description.

You can write this in a paragraph format but I'm moving toward using bullet points. They stand out more. And writing a strong paragraph is very difficult for many of us.

Value Statement Example:
- Financial oversight of companies with 10-12M yearly revenue
- Business analyst for Shell Oil
- Brought internal audits from 6 months behind to current status
- Found $9K & $13K credits sitting on the books
- Negotiated with vendors for monies owed to the company
- Initiated twice daily purchasing to improve product turnaround

Relevant Strengths Summary

This section can also be called "Relevant Skills" or "Core Expertise". This is a list of relevant certificates, knowledge, skills and traits you have for the job you're applying for. If you want to know what strengths you should emphasize, take a close look at the posted position description. If you're applying for an un-posted position, you might look for similar postings or look up the type of job in *O*NET* (www.onetonline.org). Structure the list so it's easier to read for the hiring manager.

Strengths Summary Example:

STRENGTHS SUMMARY

Certificates: Certified Public Accountant | Certified Internal Auditor

Knowledge: Payables | Receivables | Purchase Orders | Payroll

Software: Excel | QuickBooks | Peachtree | JD Edwards | Great Plains

Skills: Ledger Analysis | Revenue Recognition | Balance Sheets

Traits: Accurate | Organized | Service | Listener | Confidentiality

Resume Work Experience

This is where your "professional experience" should be listed in reverse-chronological order, starting with the most recent example. For each entry, give your position, company, the start and end date, a quick summary of what your most relevant tasks were, and a quick list of your most significant achievements. **Add quantifying numbers or metrics when possible.**

Work Experience Example:

WORK HISTORY

Accountant, Visalia, CA   04/2013 – Present
(Central Valley Business Services)
- Structuring files for businesses and land ownership
- Setting up spreadsheets and analysis for over 75 clients
- Identifying direct, indirect, repeating and variable costs

Finance Manager, Kingsburg, CA   06/2003 – 11/2012
(Western Pathology)
- Conducted audits and year-end inventory for 5 departments
- Initiated formal purchasing process
- Brought internal audits from 6 months behind to a current status

Analyst, Fresno, CA   07/2000 – 06/2003
(Data Central)
- Updated contract labor information in JD Edwards
- Setup strategic schedule for analyzing product inventory
- Created spreadsheet tracking, purchasing and finance interaction

Resume Education Section

All you need to do is list your degree or certificate, the program area and the graduation year. You may wish to list the span of years you attended.

If you have little to no experience, you may want to place your education ahead of work experience although most hiring managers surveyed don't prefer this. If you decide to go this route, you may also give a more detailed account of your coursework, major projects, internships, extra-curricular activities, and so on. Just make sure you limit what's included to what is relevant to the job you're applying for.

Education Example:

EDUCATION

B.S., Accounting, California State University   2015
Fresno, CA, GPA 3.8

Do **Not** Include References

A few years ago it was fairly common to include references as part of your resume. It was also common to use the phrase, "References Available Upon Request". This is now considered "old school" and I don't recommend it. References are just assumed in today's world. Bring a separate sheet with you to the interview. I have a reference sheet example that is fairly unique and should help you stand out. To be perfectly clear, you should not have references or mention them on your resume. Just bring them to the interview.

I have one more piece of advice on format. Never use a template provided by *Microsoft Word*, *Apple Pages* or other word processors. Applicant Tracking Software programs often have problems with these templates. They sometimes jumble the information or just don't read it. If you like the look of a template, you may reassemble it in another document without the template boxes.

Resume Samples

On the next page you can see an assembled sample of a generic resume with explanations as place holders. On the page after that is the resume I just put together for a candidate in the accounting field.

FIRST LAST

City, ST Zip | 805.555.5555 | firstlast@gmail.com | LinkedIn

Target Position (As Posted)

Specialty | Specialty | Specialty | Specialty

- Describe strengths/contributions w/ keywords from position description
- Describe strengths/contributions w/ keywords from position description
- Describe strengths/contributions w/ keywords from position description
- Describe strengths/contributions w/ keywords from position description
- Describe strengths/contributions w/ keywords from position description

STRENGTHS SUMMARY

Certificates: Certificate | Certificate | Certificate

Knowledge: Expert-Keyword | Expert-Keyword | Expert-Keyword

Software/Tools: Tool-Keyword | Tool-Keyword | Tool-Keyword

Skills: Skills-Keyword | Skills-Keyword | Skills-Keyword

Traits: Trait-Keyword | Trait-Keyword | Trait-Keyword | Trait-Keyword

WORK HISTORY

Job Title, Company, City, ST   mm/yyyy – mm/yyyy
(Description of company/industry)
- <Action word accomplished what> by <doing what> by using <list tool/tech>
- <Action word accomplished what> by <doing what> by using <list tool/tech>
- <Action word accomplished what> by <doing what> by using <list tool/tech>

Job Title, Company, City, ST   mm/yyyy – mm/yyyy
(Description of company/industry)
- <Action word accomplished what> by <doing what> by using <list tool/tech>
- <Action word accomplished what> by <doing what> by using <list tool/tech>
- <Action word accomplished what> by <doing what> by using <list tool/tech>

Job Title, Company, City, ST   mm/yyyy – mm/yyyy
(Description of company/industry)
- <Action word accomplished what> by <doing what> by using <list tool/tech>
- <Action word accomplished what> by <doing what> by using <list tool/tech>
- <Action word accomplished what> by <doing what> by using <list tool/tech>

EDUCATION

College Degree, Program,   mm/yyyy
School Name, City, ST, (GPA 3.6/4.0 - 98% Attendance)

Coursework, Program, School, City, ST,   mm/yyyy

Certificate, Company, City, ST   mm/yyyy

FIRST LAST

City, ST Zip | 805.555.5555 | firstlast@gmail.com | LinkedIn

Capital Management Specialist

Accounting | Statistics | Business Management | Compliance

- Financial oversight of companies with 10-12M yearly revenue
- Business analyst for Shell Oil
- Brought internal audits from 6 months behind to current status
- Found $9K & $13K credits sitting on the books
- Negotiated with vendors for monies owed to the company
- Initiated twice daily purchasing to improve product turnaround

STRENGTHS SUMMARY

Certificates: Certified Public Accountant | Certified Internal Auditor

Knowledge: Payables | Receivables | Purchase Orders | Payroll

Software: Excel | QuickBooks | Peachtree | JD Edwards | Great Plains

Skills: Ledger Analysis | Revenue Recognition | Balance Sheets

Traits: Accurate | Organized | Service | Listener | Confidentiality

WORK HISTORY

Accountant, Visalia, CA   04/2013 – Present
(Central Valley Business Services)
- Structuring files for businesses and land ownership
- Setting up spreadsheets and analysis
- Identifying direct, indirect, repeating and variable costs

Finance Manager, Kingsburg, CA   06/2003 – 11/2012
(Western Pathology)
- Conducted audits and year-end inventory
- Initiated formal purchasing process
- Brought internal audits from 6 months behind to a current status

Analyst, Fresno, CA   07/2000 – 06/2003
(Data Central)
- Updated contract labor information in JD Edwards
- Setup strategic schedule for analyzing product inventory
- Created spreadsheet tracking, purchasing and finance interaction

EDUCATION

B.S., Accounting, California State University   2015
Fresno, CA, GPA 3.8

Resume Keywords

Keywords are a critical component of the modern targeted resume. They should be sprinkled throughout the document. Even if the company you're applying to isn't using Applicant Tracking Software, the chances are good that the hiring manager will scan your resume looking for them.

When coming up with a list of keywords to include on your resume, the first place to look is on the position description the company has posted. You should be able to see requirements and preferences including education, certificates, skills, knowledge and traits or talents. Sometimes you will see something mentioned more than once in the position description. This should be a clue that it's important. Next, check out the company website. You can find important values and culture clues. Research the *LinkedIn* profiles of people with similar jobs to the one you're applying for.

The easiest place to embed or place the keywords, is in the Added Value Summary at the top and the following Relevant Strengths section of your resume. If you use a keyword in the Work History section, do it in an "Action-Accomplishment" or "Activity-Result" format. Use a keyword to explain your activities and resulting accomplishment.

Position Description Deconstruction/Decode

The Ladders is a popular website specializing in upper income openings and job search advice. They reported an eye tracking study showing that the average time a job candidate spent looking at a job posting or position description was between 49.2 and 76.7 seconds. This isn't enough. You may want to go through the position description underlining or highlighting keywords. Colored pens can also be helpful. Notice the underlined words below. You would want to sprinkle them in your resume.

Title: Accounting Specialist
Status: Full Time
Job Location: Fresno, CA

The Opportunity

• Are you a perfectionist?
• Are you detailed and accurate?
• Does your personal touch produce the highest quality service?
• Are you a logical, analytical thinker with an eye for proofing numerical reports?
• Do you take a systematic approach to problem solving?
• Do you have a proven ability to learn technology quickly and navigate programs with ease?

Description

Central Management Services is hiring an energetic Finance Officer to join a fast paced, growing company in California's Central Valley. The Finance Officer at Central Management works directly with clients in the office. Duties include, but are not limited to, scheduling, updating spreadsheets, development of reports, billing, procedures, and communicating directly with vendor companies.

Requirements

Qualified candidates should have experience with bookkeeping, accounting and finance. Familiarity and knowledge of multiple accounting software a plus! Qualified candidates will have strong knowledge of accounting terminology used in a construction office setting. Good communication skills, organization skills and detailed accuracy are critical! Proficiency with Microsoft Word, Microsoft Excel, and Microsoft Windows XP is mandatory. Candidates are expected to be self motivated and be able to complete given tasks and assignments as directed and within specified time constraints. Bachelors Degree in either accounting and business preferred. Compensation based on experience.

This exercise can be done in different ways. Find a way to tear the position description apart and **craft your resume in terms of the employer's interest**. Stephen Covey says that all effective people, **"Seek First to Understand, Then to Be Understood."**

Use highlighters or colored pens. You can also make a list of the company's requested qualifications with a parallel list of how you match it. If this is done really well, it can be used as a **post interview leave behind** or a document you can send or bring in a multiple interview situation.

This exercise allows you to communicate your qualifications as they meet the company preferences. It also showcases your thinking ability and may actually help the company clarify what type of candidate they are looking for.

Requested Qualifications	My Qualifications
Skills •Scheduling •Updating Spreadsheets •Development of Reports •Billing •Microsoft Office – Word & Excel	**Skills** • • • • •
Knowledge • Accounting Terms • Construction Terms	**Knowledge** • •
Attitudes •Self Motivated •Work Independently •Quality Orientation	**Attitudes** • • •
Traits •Detailed •Accurate •Perfectionist	**Traits** • • •
Education •Degrees-Accounting & Business	**Education** •
Experience •Accounting & Finance	**Experience** •

Resume Length

For introductory positions, I highly recommend keeping your resume to a single page. As you move into middle management opportunities, you will probably want to extend the length to two pages. Some positions require CV's or a curriculum vitae. These are often much longer.

You want your resume to communicate in a **10 second reading** because that's the amount of time most hiring managers will spend.

Resume Verbs

Especially in the work history or professional experience section, you want to begin each bulleted phrase with a verb. This type of writing is unique to resumes.

Job Title, Company, City, ST   mm/yyyy – mm/yyyy

(Description of company)

- <Action word accomplished what> by <doing what> by using <list tool/tech>
- <Action word accomplished what> by <doing what> by using <list tool/tech>
- <Action word accomplished what> by <doing what> by using <list tool/tech>

Verb Use Example:

Service Representative, Fresno, CA   04/2013 – Present

(Ron's Self Storage)

- Organized weekly reports on product success using *Sales Tracks*
- Created new customer satisfaction system in *Excel* Spreadsheet
- Updated accurate prices for purchases in *Transaction Manager*

Invisible "I" Format

Resume space is valuable. Almost all professional resume writers advise against using any personal pronouns. It can sound boastful, waste space and it's not really considered part of the resume writing norms. Resumes are to be written in a first person simple present or past tense with an invisible "I" format or style.

Example:

I managed day-to-day operations in the office

Should become...

Managed day-to-day operations in the office

Present or Past Tense

Present tense should usually be used when describing current duties where you are still employed. Past tense is used when describing past employment experience.

Present Tense Example:

Managing day-to-day operations in the office

Past Tense Example:

Managed day-to-day operations in the office

Adding Numbers

Professional resumes should include numbers, percentages and quantified results whenever they are available

- Increased sales 20% by implementing a new presentation
- Improved test scores by 15%
- Generated customer service scores of 4.9 out of 5.0

You'll want to begin quantifying and recording the results you create as early as possible in you career. Below is a list of the type of outcomes you'll want to begin tracking:

Accumulated Credentials
Audit Findings
Billable Hours
Budget Oversight Size
Cases Managed or Closed
Clients Acquired
Client Retention
Complaints Resolved
Cost Reduction
Cost Savings
Customer Satisfaction Scores
Customer Service Rating
Donation Increase
Employee Retention
Employees Managed
Hours Worked
Location Store Volume
Loss Prevention Reduction
Overtime Reduction
Page View Increase
Profit Increase
Projects Completed

Response Time
Safety Violation Reduction
Sales Increase
Staff Morale Numbers
Test Score Improvement

Font Style

There are generically four font types, serif, sans serif, script and decorative. There are actually a lot more than four types if you want to take a deeper dive. Go to http://en.wikipedia.org/wiki/List_of_typefaces to find explanations and examples of different fonts. But for our purposes, I will stay with the four. Serif fonts have small lines or flares that protrude from the font. Sans Serif are clean fonts that don't have the lines or flares. Script fonts roughly simulate handwriting and decorative fonts are well, decorative.

Arial is a sans serif font

Tahoma is another sans serif font

Georgia is a serif font

Times New Roman is a serif font

Bradley Hand is a script font

Broadway is a decorative font

I strongly recommend that you use a very common serif or sans serif font. Many older Applicant Tracking Software programs do not read a wide variety of fonts. If you want to stay super safe, I recommend staying with either Arial or Times New Roman.

There is some research that suggests people age 40 and younger, prefer cleaner sans serif fonts and people beyond age 40 tend to prefer serif fonts. You might wish to use that information in your resume customization. If you have a very good eye for design, you might consider mixing a serif and sans serif font in one resume but most people don't do this well.

Font Size

All content should usually be kept in the same size with headings or titles slightly larger. I recommend staying with fonts in the 10 to 12 point range. In most cases, you can use a larger font for your name.

These are Arial font point examples:

18 Point

16 Point

14 Point

12 Point

11 Point

10 Point

9 Point

These are Calibri font point examples:

18 Point

16 Point

14 Point

12 Point

11 Point

10 Point

9 Point

Notice that even though they are the same point size, Calibri appears smaller. Different fonts also use different spacing distances between letters. If you are having trouble filling a page or getting your information on one page, you can play with font styles and adjust spacing.

Color

I strongly recommend against color unless you are applying for a creative job and you are showing off your design skills.

Resume Review

Your resume is a marketing piece designed to clearly communicate your strengths and how you will make a contribution. The resume's purpose is to do one thing, get you the interview. Beyond that, in the case of a close competition, it could become a tie-breaker.

First craft a strong master resume. From that master, create customized targeted resumes for specific job openings. A good resume should be easy to read for both man and machine. And remember the 10-second rule. That's all most hiring managers will spend reading your marketing tool. You have to communicate a lot in a little space.

Cover Letters

Cover letters are still relevant and for some hiring managers, more important than the resume. It gives you a chance to describe clearly and concisely in your own words why you believe you are a good fit for the job. It also provides another opportunity to show off your writing ability and attention to detail. Like the resume, the cover letter must be well edited and completely free of errors!

Here is a generic example that can be easily adapted for your own use.

Your Name
LinkedIn ♦ 805.555.1234 ♦ name@email

Date

To: Company Hiring Manager
Re: Name of Position In Job Description

I want to express my strong interest in the _____position at _____.
My combined _____, _____, and _____
experience/education might be a good foundation to help _____ at this
position.
Please allow me to briefly detail my qualifications as they match your posted job
description requirements:

-
-
-
-

If my qualifications look like a potential fit after viewing my resume, I would love
to interview for this position. Thanks so much for your consideration.

Sincerely,

Your Name
805.555.1234
name@email

Reference Sheet

I've said this elsewhere but I will repeat it – DO NOT WRITE "REFERENCES AVAILABLE ON REQUEST" at the bottom of your resume. The phrase dates you as old school and it is assumed that you will have written references.

On the next page you'll find a sample reference sheet that I often call "References Plus". Most job applicants provide names and phone numbers and that's it. **With the "References Plus," you offer more contact information and more context and how you know the person.** It will help the reference checker ask better questions. It also displays your courtesy, thoroughness and attention to detail.

In this day and age it's rare for a company not to call for references. They've had too many bad hiring experiences and they will do everything they can not to repeat that.

Most companies are going to call at least two of your references. However, a very detailed set of references like the ones I offer as an example on the next page, may reduce the likelihood of calls or the number called.

The standard number of references requested by an employer has been three. I recommend including five. This demonstrates that you are a potentially phenomenal candidate, not just a good one.

YOUR NAME

Street Address ♦ City, State Zip ♦ Phone ♦ Email

Reference Name

Company – Phone - Email

_____ can speak from first-hand knowledge concerning my achievements as a _____and _____ in his/her district. In this capacity I reported to him/her directly. We also collaborated heavily as district managers in the Western United States. She/He has personal knowledge of my talents, skills and character.

Reference Name

Company – Phone - Email

_____ can speak from first-hand knowledge concerning my achievements as a _____ and _____. We worked together as _____ for over __ years.

Reference Name

Company – Phone - Email

_____ can speak from first-hand knowledge concerning my achievements as _____ where we served as _____ for over ___years. He/She can also attest to my skills and philosophy of _____, _____, _____ and _____. We worked together for over ___ years in varied professional relationships.

Reference Name

Company – Phone – Email

_____ and I served for ___ years together at two non-profit organizations. We co-lead _____on a number of occasions and served on _____and _____team together. He/She had a chance to observe my work with _____around _____.

Reference Name

Company – Phone – Email

_____ is a personal reference that I have known for ___ years. He/She is familiar with my work at_____, and has a familiarity with _____.

Resume Packages

To review, a complete resume package will include several pieces if you want to **stand out** from other candidates and increase your chances of getting hired. The pieces may include:

- Master resume
- Targeted resume customized to a specific position
- Master cover letter
- Targeted cover letter customized to a specific position
- Reference sheet with contact information
- Endorsement sheet with brief comments on your work
- Reference letters from co-workers, customers and employers
- Interview leave behind
- Portfolio which may include all of the above plus
  target position description, certificates, school transcripts and work samples

Every resume and every resume package should be a unique one-of-a-kind set of documents!!!

A resume package is an ongoing living description of who you are, your special strengths, what you can contribute and how you add value!

Keep your resume package updated and customize it for the specific role and specific company you are applying into.

The generic one-size-fits-all resume is dead! Please re-read that statement until it sinks into your subconscious.

This change occurred slowly. Years ago a resume was assembled with a description of work history and was delivered by mail or often brought with you to the initial interview. Most people would use the same resume regardless of what position they were applying for. Progressively, the computer has driven the change. Today, word processors like *Microsoft Word* allow almost anyone to customize their resume for a specific job opening relatively quickly. Over time it has become the norm. In other words, <u>customization is expected</u>.

Robert Half International suggests, "Rather than creating a standard document that you submit to every company that interests you, tailor your resume to each opportunity. Use the job description as your guide, emphasizing your background and abilities that closely match what the company is looking for. This may mean placing more focus on your 'certifications' and 'strong presentation skills' for one perspective employer, while playing up your 'self-directed' nature and 'proven ability to be effective with minimal supervision' for another."

Every time you deliver a resume, either electronically, by mail or in person, it should be customized.

"So often we can forget what an interview's all about. It sure feels like it's all about you, but it's really not. An interview is actually about how you can help your future boss and future employer succeed. It's about finding out what their requirements and hopes are and matching up your background and experience with what they need."

~Marc Cenedella, Founder of *"The Ladders"* Job Search

Chapter 4
Your Signature Interview

Your purpose in the job interview is to clearly communicate your strengths and how they can make a contribution to the organization in the role you are a candidate for.

How Do You Land?

Go back to the chapter titled, *Your Signature Strengths*. Review the section on *Personality*. I can come across cool and intense, especially if I'm stressed or out of my comfort zone. I also have a natural shy streak. I work on being approachable, warm and relaxed. I want you to be authentic on your interview. But I want that to always be your Best Version. You will also want to look for ways to align with the style of your interviewer(s), assess the needs of the business unit, offer alternatives and real business solutions, answer questions and ask for the job.

Just like there are job coaches all over the country helping people prepare for interview questions, there are hiring coaches all over the country helping companies do a better job identifying quality candidates. This has led to a number of creative interview approaches. Some are listed below:

Screening Interview – This pre-interview is often by phone.

Informal Un-Structured Interview – Not very planned.

Resume Interview – Asks questions about specifics on the resume.

Structured Interview - Very scripted and usually feels formal.

Behavioral Interview – Asks candidate to provide specific examples of behaviors and skills. "*Tell me about a time when* you………"

Situational Judgment Interview – Asks candidate to provide specific answers to how they would respond to a hypothetical scenario. "*What you would do if……………?*"

Case Study Interview – Offers information about a client or customer along with a request to provide sequenced details of how you'd handle them.

Strengths Interview – "*What activities do you have a natural talent for and enjoy?*"

Google Interview - Tricky mind bender questions to see how you solve problems.

Microsoft Interview - Similar to the *Google* , "*Why are manhole covers round?*"

One Question Interview – "*What project or task is your most significant accomplishment?*" (Lou Adler teaches this interview strategy to hiring managers and human resource departments all over the country.)

Work Sample/Audition Interview - Demonstrate specific skills.

Panel Interview - Usually 3 or more interviewers who rotate asking questions.

Peer Group Interview - With prospective co-workers to access group/team fit.

Group Interview - With multiple interviewees being interviewed in the same room.

Tilt-A-Whirl - Multiple interviewing stations where employees ask pre-assigned questions.

Lunch/Dinner/Golf Interview - To see how well you handle social situations.

Skype Interview - Online with video cameras or on the computer.

Stress Interview - Questions designed to make you feel uncomfortable.

The following interviews are very rare:

Sticky Situation - *"If you caught a colleague cheating on his expenses, what would you do?"*

Putting You On the Spot - *"How do you feel this interview is going?"*

Popping the Balloon - (deep sigh) *"Well, if that's the best answer you can give ..."* (shakes head) *"Okay, what about this one ...?"*

Oddball Question - *"What would you change about the design of the hockey stick?"*

Doubting Your Veracity - *"I don't feel like we're getting to the heart of the matter here."*

Start Again - *"Tell me what really makes you tick."*

Interviews that are becoming more common:

Video Interview - Upload your answers to questions asked in an online program.

Text Interview - Some companies are replacing the initial phone interview with a text conversation.

Organization Research

"Employers consider research a reflection of your interest, enthusiasm, intelligence and commitment."
~ Joyce Lain Kennedy

Robert Half CEO Max Messmer says, "Interviewers expect that you will come to the interview knowing something about the company. Not knowing enough about the company or position, displaying a bad attitude or inquiring about compensation prematurely can all leave a negative impression with hiring managers. For job seekers, the interview represents a time to shine. Thorough preparation -- including researching the employer, rehearsing responses to common questions and understanding appropriate topics to discuss -- is the key to avoiding potential pitfalls."

Research shows you are interested in the job.

Research helps you identify a bad job fit or company fit in advance.

Research allows you to have more confidence.

Research allows you to confidently answer a common interview question. Many interviewers will ask, "What do you know about our company?" It should be embarrassing for you to say, "Not very much" or have to fake an answer.

Research is the basis for the questions you will ask in the interview.

Research gives you a competitive edge against other candidates.

Organization Research Basics

Organization Website – I recommend printing off select pages and in some cases bringing them to the interview.

Google **Search** – Do a simple search and see what pops up.

LinkedIn **Search** – See if you can get an idea of the management structure. Sometimes you can figure out who the hiring manager will be and get an idea of their background and preferences.

Glass Door **Search** – This website posts interview questions commonly asked by a company.

Walk in Other Locations and Ask – If a company has multiple locations, do some research in the location you are not applying to. You might do an informational interview at an out-of-town location.

American City Business Journals at www.bizjournals.com - This business magazine offers good insight into small and medium size companies.

Parking Lot Stake Out – Get an idea of the dress code and company style.

At a minimum, you should know:

Year Founded:

Founders/CEO Name:

Reputation/Brand:

Company Style/Culture:

Interview Dress for Success

It's likely that the first judgment an interviewer will make about your professional judgment will have something to do with dress or appearance. According to recent research reported in *Forbes* magazine, people assess your competence and trustworthiness in a **quarter of a second** (250 milliseconds) based solely on how you look. In the computer age, this process starts before you even walk in the door for an interview. In many cases, recruiters and hiring managers are likely to look you up online before they even call you for an interview. The rule of thumb for interview dress is to match the existing culture for the company where you're applying or go to the interview dressed one step above the culture. You may want to discreetly discover the age of the person or persons who will be interviewing you. The recommendations below are old school and based on Boomer or Silent Generation sensibilities. If you're being interviewed and hired by a Millennial, update what I've written below.

Pant Length - Make sure your pants are tailored to match your shoe heel. The challenge is a little different for men and women. Men do wear different heels but women wear a greater variation in heels. Women also wear skirts where the heel is removed from play. The general rule of thumb is this: The hem of your dress pants should fall about ½ inch from the ground in the back—short enough that the hem doesn't drag on the ground, but long enough that the pants graze the very top of your shoe in the front.

Skirt/Dress Length – At the knee or below the knee.

Sleeve Length - Sleeves that are too long or too short can make you look unpolished. The cuff of your sleeve should hit just below your wrist when holding your arms at your sides.

Shirts/Blouses - Shirts and blouses should fit. Sometimes women struggle with blouses that gape open and men struggle with shirts that fit like a tent.

Shoes - Scuffs are the primary problem, but worn down heels look unprofessional as well. Another issue are heels that click or clatter on a hard surface. Don't show up in taps unless you're auditioning for dance.

Belts - If you have belt loops, make sure you wear a belt and make sure it is a dress belt, not a casual belt. Conversely, if your pants don't have loops, a belt is probably a bad idea unless you have a way to make sure it stays in place.

Accessories - It's best to stick with simple accessories unless you're applying for a job where you will be selling stylish accessories. In most cases, men probably shouldn't wear jewelry at all with the exception of a wedding ring. Women should probably stick with one simple earring on each ear, a maximum of one ring on each hand and a simple necklace. If wearing a tie, make sure it's classic, not too trendy and tied with a perfect knot.

Nails - Nails should be clean and well-manicured.

Hair - Clean, dry and not too trendy.

Scent – Clean, minimalist.

The Waiting Room

You'll probably meet a receptionist before you meet the person or persons who will eventually interview you. If you show up at least 10 minutes early, as you should, you'll probably be waiting a few minutes.

Make sure you treat the receptionist well. Many times they are called in and asked for an opinion after your interview is over.

I recommend reviewing material you have printed out from the company web-site or reviewing notes on yourself. Don't just sit there looking straight ahead. Make good use of your time.

The Greeting & Seating

How you greet people reveals a lot about your confidence.

Eye Contact demonstrates positive confidence in American Culture.

A Big Smile demonstrates warmth.

Firm Handshakes demonstrate confidence and warmth. - 2 seconds **is about the right length.** Try to initiate the handshake - practice beforehand.

Introduce Yourself with an upbeat tone and energy!!!

As an interviewer shakes your hand they might initiate a greeting...

"Hi, I'm _____." or "It's nice to meet you." or "Thanks for coming in."

As an interviewee you might say...

"Hi. My name is _____." (If you haven't already said your name.)
or "Thank you for seeing me."
or "It's a pleasure to meet you."
or "It's nice to meet you too."

<u>Always</u> **wait to be shown or ask where to be seated.**

Opening Question: "Tell Me About Yourself"

99% of interviews start with *"Tell Me About Yourself"*. That doesn't mean that each interviewer is looking for the same thing when they ask this question. Some interviewers really want to hear about you because they genuinely like people. Other interviewers are already beginning to make the job fit assessment. For still others, the real question may be: <u>Can</u> you tell me about yourself? Many interviewers care less about your answer to this question and more about the confidence, enthusiasm and passion with which you answer it. A few interviewers care about your response time. The biggest mistake you could make is pausing, stalling or fumbling at the onset of your answer, thus demonstrating a lack of self-awareness and self-esteem. Another big mistake is giving an answer that goes on and on. Usually a sixty second answer will suffice. Thirty to forty five seconds is better!

Try to answer this question non-verbally with eye contact, engaging body language and energy.

Your verbal answer should be practiced to the point it doesn't sound practiced. **One alternative** is the 4 E's:

<u>E</u>xperience (10 Seconds)

1.
2.
3.

<u>E</u>ducation (10 Seconds)

1.
2.
3.

<u>E</u>xcellence/Expertise (10 Seconds)

1.
2.
3.

<u>E</u>njoy/Enthusiasm (10 Seconds)

1.
2.
3.

Write out talking points for your "Tell Me About Yourself" answer above. Or....

A second alternative would be to remember your answer with a *hidden* acronym. To memorize your "Tell Me About Yourself" answer, consider creating a memory device like an acronym. This is one I might use when applying for a management job. I wouldn't tell the interviewer the acronym but just use it to keep my answer clear, concise and on-track.

The "L.E.A.D." Acronym

Listen
I believe the first duty of leadership is to listen. I'm a good listener. I notice details...

Environment
I believe good leaders create environments where other people can thrive and succeed. So I work really hard at creating a success culture.

All-Star or A+
I believe everyone is insanely great at something. I believe everyone is an all-star at something. I visualize an A+ on everyone's forehead.

Discover - Develop - Deliver
Then I set out to help my team discover their strengths, then develop and then deliver them so they are maximizing their contribution to the organization and its clients.

The 3D Answer is **a third alternative - Do-Doing-Done.**

Scott Ginsburg at *The Ladders* suggests a 3D approach.

What you "Do" as a professional making a contribution for your clients or customers...

What you're "Doing", as in current projects and upcoming events...

What you've "Done", as in past projects, who you've worked with and how helped them...

You can play with the order or sequence on this one.

Common Interview Questions

Question: "What do you know about our organization/practice, etc?"

Use your research to assemble a short answer. Go to the organization's website. Look for history, time in business, multiple locations, leadership, specialties and brand reputation.

Question: "What are your strengths?"

Use information from the work you did in the identifying your Strengths and Selling Points section and match it up with information in the position description. If there was no posted description, find 5 posted position descriptions from other companies hiring for a similar position. You can also find information on *O*Net* that should be useful. (www.onet.com)

As suggested in the section titled, "Your Signature Strengths", think about your strengths in the following categories:

Knowledge:
Skills:
Abilities/Aptitudes:
Passion:
Personality:
Character:
Experience:

Question: "What are your weaknesses?"

This question can be tricky! Here is my advice: Be honest. Don't get clever or cute with your answer. Don't try to pass off a strength as a weakness - "I'm a perfectionist". Clearly state a weakness.

Strategy 1 - Describe your "weakness management method"
Here is an example:

"I am very detailed which can cause **a project to run late**. I have learned I have to start early and set deadlines in order to get my work out on time."

Strategy 2 - Describe a non-relevant weakness
Here is an example:

"I hate public speaking."

Public speaking is usually not thought of as relevant to information technology.

Question: "Why do you want this job?"

Talk briefly about what you enjoy and what you're good at. Describe how you see the job as a good fit.

Question: "What would co-workers say about you?"

Ask co-workers, former co-workers and people that know you well to help with this question. Their answers will give you confidence and also tell you what to work on. Over time, build a portfolio of comments from these responses. Always keep every single performance review. Ask for letters of recommendation and endorsements on *LinkedIn*.

Question: "What irritates you at work?"

The best answer is something about yourself that is not too closely related to the job you're applying for. Do **NOT** use this as an opportunity to speak negatively about a co-worker or boss. Pretend you were asked about a weakness.

Question: "What is an achievement you're proud of?"

This is a very common question. In some cases the interviewer will drill deeper with follow up questions. Have a specific example that somehow relates to the job you're applying for. You may even want to prepare an achievement explanation sheet and leave it with the interviewer. The S.T.A.R. Story format I describe later in this chapter will help you with this question.

Question: "What are your goals?"

If the job you are applying for is clearly a "starter job", it's acceptable to explain how this job is to help pay your way through school or reach other goals. If you are applying for a professional or career level job, communicate that the job you're applying for is one that you can see yourself growing in for several years. Don't answer this in a way that communicates a desire to work your way up. In some companies, like *Apple*, this is seen as a negative. In other companies, like *Chipotle*, it might be viewed as ambition. Do your homework and find out the company's philosophy. Never tell the interviewer that you want their job.

Behavioral Interview Questions

Questions: "Tell me about a time when…."

"Give an example of how you satisfied a customer situation or how you exhibited good service?"

"Tell me about a time when you had too many things to do all at once… How did you handle that?"

"Tell me about a time you had a conflict with a co-worker. How did you handle that?"

"How do you stay organized?"

"Tell me about a time you were late to work…"

"Tell me about a time you received negative feedback from a supervisor."

"Give me a time in which you had to set an important goal in the past and tell me about your success in reaching it."

"Tell me about a time when you had to make an ethical decision."

"Tell me about an average day in your last position?"

Situational Judgment Interview Questions
Questions: "What would you do if…."
"What would you do if you couldn't make it in for a shift?"

"What would you do if you saw someone stealing from the register drawer?"

"How would you handle an upset client/customer?"

"How would you handle it if you saw a co-worker doing something incorrectly?"

"What would you expect your average day in this position to be like?"

Position Specific Interview Questions
Look carefully at the job description to identify the most likely role

specific questions that may be asked.

"What are the core components of a _____?"

"Tell me about your _____ experience?"

"What certifications do you have?"

"How do you handle a problem with _____ when you can't figure out what's happening?"

"Which _____systems and software are you familiar with?"

Prepare a Sixty Second S.T.A.R. Story List

I have a list of about 40 S.T.A.R. Stories from my career. These are also referred to as *Dragon Slaying* stories by some career service professionals. It's really just a success list along with a brief explanation of how you pulled it off. I keep it on a single page to review before an interview. I may pick one or two that I think would be appropriate for the specific job I'm applying for and expand it as follows:

Setting/Situation – A single sentence description of the circumstances or situation you were in:

Task/Target/Trouble – A single sentence description of your role or part including goals to reach or problems to solve:

Action(s) – A single sentence description of the specific steps you took:

Results – A single sentence description of the positive outcome:

I recommend practicing your dragon slaying S.T.A.R. story several times. You may get asked for more details but make sure you can summarize it in 4 sentences and no more than 60 seconds. You may want to turn your S.T.A.R. story into a S.T.A.R.S. story. You can make it more Strengths Oriented by adding another "S" at the end. Add a sentence summarizing the strengths you used. Talk about your passion, talent and skills specifically. If the story showcases a value you hold, you might share that.

Mock Interview

I recommend preparing some talking points like those found on the next page. Use them to practice your interviewing skills with a partner or friend. If the company is fairly large, you will be able to research their questions on *Glass Door*. Consider using an interview practice site like *Interview 4* or *Interview Stream*. Unless you have an extremely good memory, take the talking points with you to the interview.

Interview Talking Points

Position Description Qualifications	Tell Me About Yourself	Why Are You Interested In This Position?
What Are Your Greatest Strengths?	What Are Your Weaknesses?	What Would Co-Workers Say About You?
What Irritates You At Work?	What Is Your Proudest Achievement?	What Do You Know About Our Company?
What Are Your Goals?	Questions For Me? Average Work Day? Traits of Success? Appropriate Dress? Training Program? What should I ask?	Interest Statement Based on what you've said, I think I would be a good fit. What is the next step? May I have one of your business cards?

The Un-Asked Questions

As you consider and prepare for the questions that will be asked in an interview, think about some questions that won't be asked. These are questions that won't be asked directly, but they are almost always on the mind of the person who will hire you. Therefore, you'll want to provide answers. That doesn't mean you will go through each one with a well-formed summary. You will answer them in how you come across, what you wear, your attitude and so forth.

1. How will this person fit in here? This is a values and cultural fit question.

2. Will this person make me (the hiring manager) look good?

3. Will this person be hard to manage?

4. Will they make my life harder or easier?

5. How long will they stay?

6. Are they likely to bring a law suit?

7. Does this person "need" the job?

8. Will this person help me reach goals the company set?

9. Are they dependable and trustworthy?

10. What are the risks?

11. Does the candidate reflect my/our philosophy?

12. Does this candidate embrace teamwork?

13. Does this candidate take initiative?

14. Will I have to constantly give direction?

15. Does the candidate make good decisions?

16. Is this person in a protected status?

The last question is painful for many people. It's the elephant in the room… Age, Ethnicity, Gender, Disability, Orientation, Weight, Health? If there are laws that will make it more difficult to release you, some employers would prefer to not hire you. This is a terrible Catch-22 and I don't have all the answers. What I do believe is that every adversity carries with it the seed for a greater benefit. You can turn that disadvantage into an advantage. The key is to become world class at what you do. When you get clear on your strengths and select career targets based on what you're passionate about and talented for, these issues become advantages.

Prepare An Interview Portfolio

A portfolio is a grouping of evidence that showcases your preparation—examples and copies—of anything you've worked on and/or accomplished in school, at a job, or in volunteer work. For many candidates, a portfolio offers a comfortable way of demonstrating ability with "real life" examples.

According to an *American Society for Training and Development* (*ASTD*) study, people remember:

11% of what they read

20% of what they hear

52% of what they both see and hear

Portfolios have been used by many professionals to describe, display and demonstrate their developed knowledge and skill. Possible inclusions depending on your specific career target might include:

Evidence of relevant accomplishments
Achievement List
Certificates
Product Certifications
Transcripts
Technical Journals
Performance evaluations/annual reviews from past jobs
Evidence of client satisfaction
Reference letters
Work samples – **Including** *YouTube* **Videos**
Detailed challenge descriptions with solutions
Evidence of certain skills
List of technical skills such as software programs
Goals and 5-year plan
Descriptions of projects
Pictures of projects
Other relevant photos
Charts and graphs demonstrating success
Honors/Awards
Innovations
Sample training programs
Lifelong learning list
Relevant reading list

Question: "Do You Have Any Questions For Me?"

The interviewer's most critical question in a job interview is often the last one. That's when the interviewer smiles, leans forward, and says, "Now, do you have any questions for me?"

Asking just the right questions is your chance to demonstrate that you are the best candidate for the job by communicating five different impressions:

Interest – *You have taken the trouble to investigate the job*

Intelligence – *You really understand the requirements of the job*

Confidence – *You have everything it takes to do the job*

Personal appeal – *You are the type of person who will fit in well*

Assertiveness – *You ask for the job*

Always ask a minimum of 3 questions. I like the following questions:

What are the activities in an average work day?

What are the traits of other people who have performed this job successfully?

What is considered appropriate dress?

What is the initial and ongoing training program?

Is there any question I'm not asking that I should?

Your Closing Comments – Take the opportunity to reaffirm your strong interest in the position and your belief that you would be a good fit using language like:

"Based on what you just shared, I believe I would be a good fit for this job. I'm very interested."

"What is your decision making process like? What are the next steps?"

It is absolutely critical that you tell your interviewer that you want the job! The above phrases are polite ways of communicating that.

<u>**Don't Ask!!!**</u> (based on hiring manager surveys)

When can I start?
How much is the starting salary?
How many vacation days will I receive?
Can I get a voucher for parking after this interview?
What is this position for again?
Do you hire family members?
Does this company have a high turn-over rate?
Will I get paid for holidays?
When do the benefits start?
When will I be eligible for my first raise?

Curveballs

Van Halen was a top rock band that toured for many years. They had a very detailed contract that contained a "Brown *M&M*" clause. Band member David Lee Roth explained that the clause also contained a provision stating that the promoter would forfeit all pay if this clause was ignored.

What was the big deal? Was Van Halen just being difficult? Roth explained the rationale behind the contract provision. To summarize, the clause was in place to check the detail orientation and the local stage set up crew. If the band found brown *M&M's* back stage this was a tip off that the promoter had either not read the agreement or not paid attention to details. Why was that important? It was a safety issue. Van Halen toured with a set of 850 lights. This required special stage trusses and electrical considerations. Lighting could collapse and electrical system overloads could occur. The band was confident that if the brown *M&M* issue was handled properly, the safety issues would be handled as well. If the band showed up and found brown *M&M's* back stage, they immediately checked every detail of the staging. What does this have to do with interviews? A lot!!! They are an opportunity to display:

A Sense of Humor
Flexibility
Imagination
Thinking on Your Feet
How You Think or Solve Problems

They may also be attempts to understand a candidate's:

Sense of Detail
Ability to Follow Directions
Work as Part of a Team

The following are examples of questions or requests that are currently happening at interviews. In each case, I either witnessed it personally or was debriefed by some who had direct knowledge:

Application Requests With A Job Description

Consider the following real job description:

You will be a front-line representative, in charge of delivering exceptional customer service to clients. You will take inbound calls, explain how the program works, help potential customers sign up, review account status, provide guidance on product features, re-enforce product value to retain current customers and ensure customer satisfaction.

We are looking for out-going people who are super-friendly and have great attitudes!

The main responsibility of the Customer Service Representative is to provide prompt, friendly, and accurate support for cardholders. This role requires the ability to resolve customer inquiries, escalate as needed, follow up with customers, and multitask on related activities. You will be the face and voice of this company. You will need to listen carefully to what the customer is saying while maintaining a super-friendly, polite and helpful attitude.

We are a growing company and this is a growth opportunity for the right candidate. **So that I know you read this, please start the first line of your cover letter with the sum of the numbers five and two. Your email will not reach us if you don't follow this exact instruction.**

(The company that wrote this job description did not underline or place the request in bold. The candidate that I was coaching had not read the request and was about to send off her application cover letter without the required information.)

Here is another Pre-Interview Request

To apply, please send the following:

Resume
Cover Letter
A short story that demonstrates that you are super-friendly.

(When asked to write something as part of your application process, always have someone proofread your writing for grammar and spelling.)

Curveball Interview Scenarios

The following are interview scenarios that my clients have faced:

Interview Request: You have 15 minutes to design a creative resume. You can use no words. (Flip chart size paper was supplied with colored markers.)

4-Hour Work Sample Interview: Some companies are paying candidates to come in and work an actual shift as part of the interview or selection process.

4-Hour, 9-Person, Panel Interview: Some companies are conducting very lengthy interviews with multiple staff present and asking questions. (I spoke with a candidate who answered questions from nine people for four hours. This was an introductory position.)

Interview - 1 Leader, 12 Observers, 16 Interviewees Divided Into Teams of 4... Toy animals were on each table for team mascots. Candidates were asked to build a tower with index cards and tooth picks. Colored pens and index cards for name decoration were provided. Each candidate was given 20 seconds to introduce themselves and why they chose that decoration. A bell signaled the end of the 20 seconds. The interview leader asked questions that included:

What are the most populous countries?

What are the top 10 animals that cause human death?

What are the top 10 grossing movies?

There was a math quiz that involved money.

Logic questions were included.

Math word problems were included.

Ten names were assigned to put in alphabetical order.

Candidates were asked to write two complete sentences describing the week's weather.

Prizes included bags of candy, bouncing balls and *Dollar Store* items.

Wine and cheese was served at the end. The interview was 1.5 hours start to finish including a facility tour.

Curveball Questions

What's the color of money?

Are you a hunter or gatherer?

Why is a tennis ball fuzzy?

What is the funniest thing that happened to you recently?

How lucky are you? Why do you say that?

You're a new crayon addition to the box. What color are you and why?

What is your least favorite thing about humanity?

If you could create a parade through the company office, what type of parade would it be?

What is the last gift you gave someone?

Describe the process and benefits of wearing a seatbelt.

If you were a pizza delivery person, how would you use scissors?

How many square feet of pizza are eaten in the U.S. each year?

How many snow shovels were sold in the U.S. last year?

If you could sing one song on *The Voice*, what would it be?

How honest are you?

It's Thursday and we're staffing you on a telecommunications project in Calgary, Canada on Monday. Your flight and hotel are booked and your passport is ready. What are the top 5 things you do before you leave?

If you were on an island and could only bring three things, what would you bring?

Do you believe in Big Foot?

How would you instruct someone to make an origami "cootie catcher" using only words?

If you were a box of cereal, what would you be and why?

If you were 100 years old, what would be the best single piece of advice you would give?

How would you use *Yelp* to find the number of businesses in the U.S.?

Think about answering these questions in such a way that demonstrates a skill or quality you have that qualifies you for the job. If you are asked, "what color best represents you?", you might say, "blue, because it is a calming color, and I am good at staying calm under pressure." ... Or.... "A rainbow, because I'm good at shifting colors based on the need."

If you could not answer the question by the end of the interview, include a response to the question in your follow up or thank you note/email.

Interview Follow Up

Thoughtful post-interview communication underscores the traits that companies are looking for. Being able to convey what they could bring to the position can give certain job seekers a significant advantage over less-proactive candidates. According to a survey reported by *CareerBuilder*, by not sending a thank you note:

22% of employers are **less likely to hire** a candidate.
86% of employers say it **shows a lack of follow-through**.
56% of employers say the **candidate isn't really serious** about the job.

If you are interviewed by three people... Send three separate notes.

Each situation is different, but here are some content suggestions:

Thank them for their time.

Revisit questions or points talked about in the interview.

Elaborate on a question that wasn't fully answered.

Suggest a solution or a desire to help solve a problem that was discussed.

Communicate that you want the job and why you would be a great fit.

Options (In positions requiring multiple interviews, create a strategic follow up sequence.)

Thank you note

Thank you email

Email with reference package attachment

Email with interview notes

Email summarizing qualifications

Appropriate creative communication of additional qualifications

Phone call

Sample Interview Follow Up Email/Letter

Date

Hi _____,

I wanted to follow up after our meeting together yesterday afternoon. I appreciate the time you gave me, and I found the interview helpful as I get a better understanding of the responsibilities and required results in the _____ position.

As an additional resource, I've attached a professional reference package for your consideration. You will find 5 references with convenient contact information along with some context on our relationship history.

I hope to hear from you soon!

Thank you so much,

Your Name
Your Email
Your Cell Phone

Use A Checklist

Cell Phone Is In The Car

No Gum

Arrive 20 Minutes Early - Go In 10 Minutes Early

Use Bathroom Somewhere Else

Bottled Water/Energy Bar/Caffeine (leave in car)

Toothpick or Brush (leave in car)

Breath Mints (leave in car)

Advil or *Aspirin* (leave in car)

Directions (The GPS System Doesn't Always Work Perfectly)

Cash (For Parking, Tolls and Emergencies)

Worst Case Scenario Kit (Spot Remover, Umbrella, Band Aids)

Your Interview Kit (Items to Bring In)

A Nice Portfolio Style Binder

Samples of Relevant Work

Printed Copies Of Your Resume x3

Pad & Paper

Pen - 3x

A List of Job Related Questions

Reference Sheets

Copy of Cover Letter (If Sent)

Copy of Job Description

Copy of Job Description Deconstruction (See Resume Chapter for Details)

Always Show Up!

"80% of success is showing up."
~Woody Allen

I worked as a hiring manager on the West Coast for 8 years interviewing candidates from Seattle to San Diego and a lot of places in between. If I had 10 candidates on the schedule for interviews any given day, the show up rate was around 2. Think about that. They responded to an ad and took the time to schedule an interview but only 20% of the candidates actually showed up for the interview.

One of my favorite stories comes from *Chicken Soup for The Soul – Living Your Dreams* edition. In the story titled, *The Interview*, Nicole Jenkins shares about what she called, "The job of a lifetime." Nicole says she couldn't wait for the interview. It was a position she'd dreamt of and prepared for.

On the morning of the interview, Nicole woke up and could hardly open her eyes. Her face felt stiff and contorted like she had suffered a stroke and she couldn't open her lips normally. Her eyes were misaligned and speech was slurred.

Her mother rushed her to the hospital and went through all kinds of tests. After several hours, it was determined that she had Bell's palsy.

She told the doctor about the interview and the only suggestion was to reschedule. "In a few days," he said, "your face should return to normal."

Nicole debated, but decided she was going to the interview. Her mom resisted, "Honey, I don't think you should. You look...strange."

Reluctantly her mom drove Nicole to the interview. She walked in the office and walked right up to the woman sitting at the front desk. "Nicole Jenkins to see Mr. Robertson."

The receptionist stared at her face and responded, "He's expecting you. Go right in."

Nicole was terrified, rushed in and nervously sat in the chair facing

Mr. Robertson.

"Hello," he said, "Miss Jenkins?"

"Yes. Please excuse me. I'm having a Bell's palsy attack. My doctor explained to me that it would last a few days. I came right from the hospital."

"You're a very dedicated woman to come when you're not feeling up to speed," he responded, after a pause.

"Yes, sir."

He spent a few minutes looking over the application. "Is everything on here correct?" He held it out to look at.

Nicole glanced over the paper, "Yes, but I failed to mention I type seventy-five words per minute."

"Wonderful," he smiled. "Out of one hundred points, you had our highest score on the application test. You scored well above average on grammar and computer programs."

"It comes easily for me," Nicole honestly replied.

"Well, you certainly are qualified. You have an impressive background with related experience. I see here you worked for the navy."

"Directly with legal affairs," she reiterated.

"When are you available?"

"Two weeks."

He gazed down onto his desk calendar. "The 27th then, be here at 9 A.M."

She gasped, "You're hiring me?"

"Yes, you're perfect for the position."

Nicole stood. "Thank you for believing in me. I won't let you down."

"I know," he smiled, rising from his desk to shake my hand. "Not only have you got the skills I'm looking for, you also have the character."

"Direct calling not only improves the odds of landing a job quickly, it also improves the odds of landing a good job. Direct calling is much more effective than other approaches."

~Brian Graham, Author of *Get Hired Fast!*

Chapter 5
Direct Contact and Hidden Jobs

"You will never possess what you are unwilling to pursue."
~Mike Murdock

Up to this point, we have been working on job search preparation: Identifying your job related strengths, targeting employers, crafting resume materials and preparing for interviews. Now it's time to start your job search.

There are basically 4 types of job search: **Direct Contact** - reaching out to employers who may have openings but have not posted them; applying to **Employer Postings**; building and expanding your **Relationship Network**; and establishing yourself with **Staffing Services**.

Reaching into the hidden job market with well-planned visibility contacts is the most underappreciated, yet often most effective job search method.

The "Visibility" Problem

Many job coaches believe that up to 80% of the available jobs are not posted on any job board. They are completely invisible to the average job seeker. Many of the best candidates are passive and hidden from employers and hiring managers.

How Companies Fill Jobs

Most companies prefer to fill open positions using the following 4 strategies in sequence. <u>Actually posting a job is usually last on the list.</u>

Internal Search

Networking

Resume Search

Job Posting

In fact, I've had hiring managers and human resource professionals tell me that they will do almost anything to avoid posting an opening. They are not set up to handle the influx of applications, most of which come from candidates who don't come close to the posted qualifications.

The purpose of a "Direct" Contact is **to make invisible or hidden jobs visible** and **to make an invisible or hidden candidate (You) visible.**

Why Direct Contacts Are A Strong Strategy

1. Allows you to focus on jobs that **"fit"** rather than what **"appears"** to be available (Many companies run job ads even when they are not hiring.)

2. Finds the "un-posted" job market - Up to **80% of available jobs**

3. Finds **positions about to open** before they are posted

4. Finds positions where the job **opening is still in the pipeline**

5. Finds positions where **underperformers are about to be released**

6. Finds positions where an employer doesn't want to release **hiring plans to competition**

7. Finds positions where an employer doesn't have **funds to post an opening**

8. Finds positions where an employer wants to get company **employee referrals first**

9. Finds positions where an employer hates weeding through **hundreds of resumes**

10. Finds opening under **hiring freeze conditions** that will open up shortly

11. Allows you to impress an employer who may **create a position for you**

12. Allows you to impress an employer who may **alert you to a future opening**

13. Very few job candidates do this... It takes courage!

14. It immediately sets you apart from other candidates

Types of Visibility Contact

Listed below are 6 types of direct contact methods. Strategies 1-4 are generally listed in the order of their effectiveness based on the number of repetitions required to gain an interview. This list is also ordered by the amount of courage required from the average person. In my case, I find face-to-face contacts much easier than phone contacts.

1. Direct - Targeted **Visits** (Face-to-Face)
2. Direct - Targeted **Phoning**
3. Direct - Targeted **Email**
4. Direct - Targeted **Introduction Letters/Pain Letters**
5. Direct - Targeted **Staffing Service** Contacts
6. **Combining** All The Above

Face-to-Face Approaches

(Progressively Requiring Less Courage & Skill)

Here is a list of face-to-face direct approaches that require you to walk into a location and introduce yourself. The first one on the list requires more courage and skill. Each number progressively requires less courage and slightly less skill. The effectiveness goes down exponentially.

1. Research the hiring manager by name and ask them to look at your resume

"Hi, my name is_____, is John or Mary in?"

"I'm_____... I wanted to come in and introduce myself... I know you may not have a current opening... but I was hoping you would take just a minute, look at my resume... and give me some feedback on my skills, background and experience."

2. Research the hiring manager and ask to see them by name

"Hi, my name is_____, is John or Mary in?"

3. Ask to see manager by position

"Hi, my name is_____, is the manager in?"

4. Drop off resume with the receptionist (Like leaving a brochure)

"Hi, my name is _____and I wanted to come in and drop off my resume."

5. Leave your resume on office door (<u>Not</u> very effective)

Phone Approaches

Here is a simple phone script:

Hello, my name is _____.

I would like to explore working with _____. (Company Name)

Can you tell me how you do your recruitment for _____?

Who would I talk with about that?

The Introduction Letter/Email

Sending an introduction letter or email doesn't require a lot of courage and if you develop a system, it shouldn't take too much time. Introduction letters, by themselves, are a low percentage strategy. They can be enhanced by customization, recognizing what is unique about a particular office or business unit. The results can be significantly increased if you tell the potential employer that you will be following up with a cover letter-resume package in a few days and follow that up with a phone call.

Date

Dear Mr. or Ms. Last Name,

I have 5 years experience as a _____, recently graduated from _____ and I am currently looking for a _____ position in the Central Valley.

_____ Company has been recognized as one of the top _____ professionals in the _____ specialty. You may have many applicants waiting in the wings or on file. Mine is one more, but I do offer some enthusiasm that is rare.

I am interested in an _____ position with _____ company and I hope that I can join the team.

My record is one of solid accomplishment, advancement and increasing levels of responsibility. I will forward my resume in the coming week to see if my background may be a good fit with opportunities in your organization.

Sincerely,

Your Signature

Your Typed Name
Phone
Email

The Pain Letter/Email

A pain letter or email is a particular type of introduction developed by *Human Workplace* expert Liz Ryan. Here is a four-point outline based on her invention.

The Compliment
The Pain Hypothesis
Your Story
The Closing

Dear Mr./Ms. Last Name,

(The Compliment) Congratulations on building such a successful _____company. I have reviewed your website and was amazed at the service you offer here in the Central Valley.

(Pain Hypothesis) I can imagine that as you grow, finding _____candidates who fit in your organization can be time consuming and sometimes frustrating.

(Your Story) I am a recent graduate with an _____ degree and carried a 3.91 G.P.A. and a 100% attendance record. I have a solid work history, references and a passion for this profession. Whenever it's convenient, I would love to speak with you or your hiring manager about potential future openings.

(The Closing) If you have time for a telephone call or email correspondence, I would love to share a bit more about my background.

Thank you for your consideration,

Your Signature

Your Typed Name
Phone
Email

Staffing Service Direct Contacts

I have a whole chapter (8) devoted to this topic.

Finding Employers to Build a Target List

You must create **a target list of potential employers**. I recommend building a list of 50 companies that have offices in your general area. With most jobs this is easy using *Google Maps*.

Open a web browser and then open *Google*

Go to *Google Maps*: https://www.google.com/maps

In the Search Bar at the upper left corner, simply type in the word for the type of employer who normally hires what you do. Add the name of your city or you can use a zip code.

Example: Fresno, CA Computers
Example: Los Angeles, CA Architects
Example: Sacramento, CA Builders

Open an *Microsoft Word* or *Excel* document and name it "Job Search Target List". Click on the red dots in the *Google Maps* Screen. A company that has an address at the red dot will pop up in the upper left corner. Copy and paste the address, phone number and if available, the website. Repeat until you have targets.

Repeat this process in *Google Maps* with another phrase:

Example: "Sacramento, CA Construction Companies". You may find a few more companies that didn't come up when you used the word "Builders".

Important: *Google Maps* works on a different search algorithm than a normal web search in *Google*. Usually a web search in *Google* will pull up many companies from outside your area. In this case, *Google Maps* is a much more effective approach. Once you locate the company name, you may wish to switch over to a standard *Google* web search and pull up the company web-site.

"Follow instructions in the job posting and on the application form. Failing to do so will get your application thrown away because it shows the hiring manager that you lack attention to detail."

~Michael Roberts, from *The Balance*

Chapter 6
Employer Postings

Applying For Open Positions

Applying for posted openings is one part of a well-rounded job search strategy. I recommend spending 30 minutes looking at 2 or 3 targeted sites every day. If you find something where you fill 80% of the qualifications, apply for the job. Three days is a recommended time window. Don't let a job sit. On the other hand, if a job has been posted for a while, the organization may be having trouble filling the opening. Go ahead and apply.

Finding Posted Openings

Google – http://www.google.com - *Google* is a search engine. A search can pull up job postings from a wide variety of sources. The down side is that it's difficult to target.

Indeed – http://www.indeed.com - *Indeed* is a meta-search aggregator that combs the large company websites and other job boards like *Monster* and *Career Builder* in order to repost their openings.

Craigslist – http://www.craigslist.org - Some employers only post a job on *Craigslist*. The board has legally shut off re-postings by meta-search aggregators. When a job is posted on *Craigslist* it is not likely that it will be posted anywhere else. They have excellent postings.

Niche Boards – Some job boards are dedicated to a specific area or a specific industry. One example is *Dice*, which is a very popular site for the tech industry. They should be picked up by a meta-search aggregator like *Indeed* but it is possible that a job gets missed.

Advertised Position Names

Jobs are frequently advertised <u>under a wide variety of position names</u>. For example, I work as a career development coach. But this position is called by 15 or 20 different names. Here are a few examples from my profession:

Vocational Counselor
Job Search Coordinator
Vocational Rehabilitation
Job Developer
Employment Development
Career Advisor
Career Services Director
Transition Specialist
Outplacement Counselor

Every profession goes by more than one name. You will want to develop a list of what different organizations call your role or position. To get started, go to www.onetonline.org . In the Occupation Quick Search, in the upper right hand corner, type in the name of your target job or profession. You will come to a page of positions that are loosely in your field. Click on the one that is most similar to your target. This will bring you to a page that displays a sample of reported job titles. This is a good starting list. When you use a job board, you will want to search using all the different job names.

There are downsides to applying for posted openings. First, you may be one of 250 candidates applying for a position. That is not good odds for being one of the 4-5 candidates selected for the interview. Second, many large companies buy advertising space in bulk. They often run job ads when there is not a job opening.

Application Tips

Create a "Master Application" with information that precisely matches your resume information & *LinkedIn* profile – Always make sure your application, resume and *LinkedIn* profile do not have conflicting dates. Human resource directors and hiring managers are looking for anything that might suggest dishonesty.

Proofread your application, and if possible have someone else proofread for mistakes. This is a huge advantage of applying online.

Biggest Application Mistakes

Spelling Errors

Grammatical Errors

Not Following Directions

Marking Limited Availability

Marking Limited Hours

Not Being 100% Truthful

Vague Dates In Employment History

Listing References Without Permission

Poor Penmanship (Written Applications)

On the next page is a sample application. I recommend filling out this one or something similar. Take it with you to an interview or any setting where you may be asked to fill out an application. You can also keep the information in a *Microsoft Word* document on your tablet or smart phone.

Application Form Preparation Sheet

Qualified applicants receive equal consideration. No question is asked for the purpose of securing information to discriminate against any applicant due to race, creed, color, national origin, religion, age, sex, handicap, veteran status, marital status, sexual orientation, or any other characteristic protected by law. We are an equal opportunity employer.

Personal Information

Today's Date _____

SSN ____-___-_____

Last Name _____ First Name _____ Middle _____

Address _____ City _____ State ___ Zip _____

Phone _____ Work _____ Alt _____

Are you over the age of 18? ( ) Yes ( ) No   If no, you will be required to provide authorization to work.

Are you legally eligible to be employed in the United States? ( ) Yes ( ) No Proof of identity and eligibility will be required upon employment.

Have you ever been convicted of a felony or misdemeanor? ( ) Yes ( ) No If yes, please explain _____
_____

Conviction will not necessarily disqualify an applicant from employment.

Have you ever been debarred? ( ) Yes ( ) No   If yes, when did this occur?
_____

Who was the debarring agency? _____

Employment Desired

Position applying for? _____When can you begin work? _____

What salary do you expect? _____ Can you travel if required? ( ) Yes ( ) No If yes _____%

Have you ever been employed by this Company or Affiliates before?
( ) Yes ( ) No If yes, provide details:

Company _____ Department _____ Supervisor _____

Dates employed _____to _____ Reason for termination? _____

Do you have any relatives or acquaintances that work for this company?
( ) Yes ( ) No
If yes, who are they and where do they work? _____

Have you signed any confidentiality/non-disclosure agreements with any employer? ( ) Yes ( ) No

Do you have any reason to believe that your employment with this company could constitute a breach of that agreement? ( ) Yes ( ) No
Be prepared to provide a copy of that to human resources.

How were you referred to us? ( ) Advertising ( ) Agency ( ) Internet
( ) Employee ( ) Other _____

If referred by employee, list name and location.
_____

Employment Experience

PLEASE PRINT NEATLY AND USE AN INK PEN. EXPECT EVERY PERSON TO BE CONTACTED. COMPLETE ALL AREAS. DO NOT RESPOND WITH "REFER TO RESUME".

MAY WE CONTACT YOUR CURRENT EMPLOYER? ( ) YES ( ) NO
If no, include a professional reference who may be contacted to verify current employment.

Most Recent Employer _____ **Position** _____ **Dept.** ____

Street _____ City/State/Zip _____

Employment Dates _____ to _____ Final Salary _____ per _____

Supervisor's Name _____ Phone _____

2nd Supervisor's Name _____ Phone _____

Reason For Leaving _____

Next Recent Employer _____ **Position** _____ **Dept.** ____

Street _____ City/State/Zip _____

Employment Dates _____ to _____ Final Salary _____ per _____

Supervisor's Name _____ Phone _____

2nd Supervisor's Name _____ Phone _____

Reason For Leaving _____

Next Recent Employer _____ **Position** _____ **Dept.** ____

Street _____ City/State/Zip _____

Employment Dates _____ to _____ Final Salary _____ per _____

Supervisor's Name _____ Phone _____

2nd Supervisor's Name _____ Phone _____

Reason For Leaving _____

EDUCATION

Provide a record of all high schools, colleges, universities, and special schools you have attended

Name of Institution _____ City/State _____

Did You Graduate? () Yes () No Degree_____ Major _____

Name Used During Attendance _____

Name of Institution _____ City/State _____

Did You Graduate? () Yes () No Degree_____ Major _____

Name Used During Attendance _____

Name of Institution _____ City/State _____

Did You Graduate? () Yes () No Degree_____ Major _____

Name Used During Attendance _____

SPECIAL SKILLS AND TRAINING
Summarize Job Related Skills and Training

_____

_____

_____

Days-Times Available For Employment
When Can You Work?

Mon__	Tues__	Wed__	Thurs__	Friday__	Sat __	Sun__
All__	All__	All__	All__	All__	All__	All__
Morn__	Morn__	Morn__	Morn__	Morn__	Morn__	Morn__
After__	After__	After__	After__	After__	After__	After__
Eve__	Eve__	Eve__	Eve__	Eve__	Eve__	Eve__
Night__	Night__	Night__	Night__	Night__	Night__	Night__

In the Next 3-6 Months
Will You Be Needing Time Off? If so, Explain.

_____

Application Landmines

Applications can have numerous landmines. Here are five common ones found in the sample application above.

Past Salary – Many online applications will not allow you to leave this blank. Try to keep the answer somewhere near the salary range of the position you're applying for. Anything radically higher or lower than the starting salary of the job you're applying for may raise a red flag for the employer.

Salary Expectations – Do your homework with a resource like *Glass Door*. Your expectations should be close to role and industry norms.

Confidentiality Agreements – If you have one, disclose it and bring it with you.

Day and Time Availability – When applying for a new job, don't expect special privileges. Check all the boxes. If you need to negotiate for a legitimate reason, negotiate after you get the job offer… or preferably after you've passed the 3 month probation window.

Time Off Requests – Yes I know you had the cool European vacation planned. Maybe you've already bought the plane tickets. But if you want the job, post-pone the trip until your first vacation.

"Everything great that happens in your career always starts with someone you know. You don't need to surf the net. Your next big break will not come from some mysterious technology, or discovery of new information. Your next big break will come from someone you know. Go know people."

~Derek Sivers, Founder of *CD Baby*

Chapter 7
Relationship Networking

It is critical that you <u>do not depend on your existing network of relationships</u>. If you always do what you've always done, you'll always get what you've always got. You must get outside your existing sphere of relationships and begin building a network inside the field you want to enter. Go know people!

Relationship - Reputation – Brand

"It isn't what they say about you, it's what they whisper."
~Errol Flynn

The quality of your relationships are connected to your reputation, or what you are known for. This is true in both your personal and professional life. In the professional world, your reputation, what you're known for, is often referred to as your "brand".

This is easy to recognize with large companies. What are these organizations known for? Work through the list and write a single word or single phrase answer next to each company. That answer is the company's brand, at least in your mind. It is their mindshare.

Apple

Barnes and Noble

Coca Cola

Disney

Facebook

Google

Honda

In-N-Out

McDonald's

Nike

Pepsi

Starbucks

Target

Toyota

UPS

Verizon

Walmart

Let's try the exercise with real people. This time I'll start with a description and you see if you can tell me the name.

Invented the "Moon Walk"

First person to walk on the real moon

Actress in and out of rehab… and jail

Shock Jock on the radio

Rude original judge on American Idol

Under the sea documentary film maker

Spoiled sisters who are famous for being famous

Creator of The Muppets

Now add your name and a few friends or family members. What is each individual known for? That is their brand!

What Are You Known For?
What's Your Reputation?
What Do People Remember About You?

What Do They Say When You Leave The Room?

List 3 Things You Believe You Are Known For:

1.

2.

3.

What Do You Want To Be Known For?

List 3 Things:

1.

2.

3.

"Your brand is how you arrive, how you depart and what people think, feel and remember about you after you've left the building."
~David Avrin

Reputation Builders

Your managers, co-workers and employees will remember you for...

The **Responsibilities** you shoulder

The **Results** you create

The **Relationships** you develop

What's a **Reference? (Powerful)**

Someone who agrees to <u>vouch for your credentials and qualifications</u> for a specific position when contacted by a hiring company. They may include co-workers, employees, managers, partners and customers. They may come from *LinkedIn* recommendations, letters, comment cards, emails and more.

What's a **Referral? (More Powerful)**

Someone who **initiates contact** with a hiring manager on your behalf suggesting you are a **possible strong candidate** with qualifications for a specific position.

What's a **Recommendation? (Most Powerful)**

Someone who **initiates contact** with a hiring manager on your behalf and **strongly suggests you are the perfect candidate for a specific position.**

The Recommendation Hierarchy

I've adapted this recommendation hierarchy from recruiter Lou Adler:

1. **Get recommended by an influential person who can vouch for your performance (100X)**. This is gold in the hands of a candidate, particularly if the hiring manager personally knows the referrer. This is the best way for a candidate to obtain an instant interview. It's almost as effective as being promoted internally.

2. **Get recommended by a less trusted source who can vouch for your performance (50X)**. It's hard to resist someone going out of his or her way to vouch for another person.

3. **Get recommended by an influential person even if they can't vouch for your performance (20X)**. If a hiring manager had an open spot, many would review the resume out of curiosity and if the candidate had a strong resume, they might make contact by phone or email for a phone interview.

4. **Get recommended by anyone within the company even if they don't know you too well (10X)**. In this case the quality of the referrer becomes the differentiator. The less credible, the less the referral is worth. Regardless, if the hiring manager has a need to fill the position, the person's resume would at least get to the top of the stack and be personally reviewed.

Endorsements

An endorsement is a teammate or manager who will write a few sentences, a paragraph or letter testifying to the quality of your work. Who have you worked with (teammates), or worked for (managers) that might serve as a powerful recommendation or endorsement?

List them here:

1.

2.

3.

4.

5.

6.

7.

8.

9.

10.

List Your References

Who will you ask to be a reference for your **job application** and **reference package**? Most companies request 3 and some request up to 5. I recommend at least one reference who is of a different gender (a female if you are male or a male if you are female). Try to use people that know you well and with whom you have a relationship that exceeds five years in length.

List them here:

1.

2.

3.

4.

5.

6.

7.

8.

9.

10.

Network Jump Start Sample Email

Dear Friend, Former Co-Worker, Etc...

I just wanted to drop you a note to update you on my career progress. I'm in the process of doing a very targeted job search and have been coached that one of the most effective strategies for finding the best opportunities is by networking with friends and associates.

To bring you up to date on my career, I'm enclosing a copy of my resume along with a copy of 10 positions/organizations I've been researching as potential employers. Please look over the list. If you could connect me with anyone who works in one of these companies, it could be a great help to me.

Also, if you know someone or have a connection with a similar organization, I would be grateful for his or her name. If it's comfortable and appropriate, an introduction would be awesome.

I really would appreciate your help or any ideas you might have.

Thanks so much,

Your Name
Cell Phone #
Email

Join Professional Organizations

Join professional organizations. Go to local chapter meetings and attend conferences. Build professional relationships. Go to www.meetup.com and look for meetings related to your profession. Conduct a *Google* search for professional organizations connected with your target profession.

List 3 organizations related to your profession here:

1.

2.

3.

Social Media Channels

Increasingly, your presence and active "professional" participation on social media channels are considered a critical part of an effective job search and career development. In some cases, employers are beginning to request links to a *LinkedIn* Profile instead of a resume.

I believe a well-thought-out *LinkedIn* Profile is important for anyone serious about advancing in their career. *Twitter* can be useful but I wouldn't consider it critical at this point. *Google* + is rising in influence quickly. *Facebook* has the potential as a job search vehicle but the most important thing is to keep it free of photos and other indicators that you participate in activities that are either illegal or professionally questionable.

About 80% of employers say they are now checking social media for evidence of behaviors they consider negative. This has become such a big issue that a very successful company now exists to help you clean up your *Facebook* and *Twitter* profiles. It's called *SimpleWash*.

LinkedIn

At this stage, I believe *LinkedIn* should be your primary social media concern. A well-crafted *LinkedIn* profile has many benefits. Your profile:

 • Functions as a **resume extension** that offers more in depth and compelling information

 • Provides a way to **store updated information** to include in future resumes

 • Fills out **online applications with the push of a button**

 • Allows **recruiters to forward** *a comprehensive career summary*

 • Offers an easy way to **gather endorsements & recommendations**

 • Begins **to build your online "Brand"**

 • **Over-rides negative information** on others with your same name

 • Allows recruiters to **find you**

 • **Portrays you as up-to-date** and technologically savvy

 • Allows you to easily find and **communicate with industry peers**

 • Offers an easy way to follow and **stay in touch with past co-workers**

 • Allows you to find **and track industry role models**

 • Provides a way to identify **role model career paths**

 • Allows you a way to **track industry trends** and conversations daily

 • Provides an additional way to **research potential employers**

 • Provides a way to research companies **before an interview**

For a better grasp of *LinkedIn* and its power, go to:

http://press.linkedin.com/about

How To Optimize Your *LinkedIn* Profile

The best way to optimize your profile is to find 5-7 outstanding profiles from those who already excel in the industry you hope to work in. You will want to notice how they "package" themselves and do something similar as it fits.

A *LinkedIn* profile has about 25 components, depending on how they are counted and grouped. (This changes occasionally.) *LinkedIn* has been known to add and remove components so you'll want to stay up to date. The platform is also more dynamic than a resume, meaning you should be updating and interacting with it at least weekly if not daily.

LinkedIn Components

Header

Name – Should be consistent with resume and other communications.

Headline – Refine this by looking at other professionals in your industry.

Picture – Go to a studio and have it professionally done. (white or black background)

Header Information – Model others in your industry.

Connections – Set a goal of 500 contacts, mostly in your industry.

Contact Information – Set up an email link, possibly a phone number or a consistent way to communicate.

Background

Summary – Read several summaries used by peers or role models and modify.

Presentations – *Vimeo, YouTube, Slide Share* Etc…

Experience – This section is similar to a resume but it has room for more information. Include stats and achievements.

Education – Include more **professionally relevant** details than you ever would on your resume.

Certifications – Include all **professionally relevant** licenses and certificates.

Courses – Include all **professionally relevant** seminars, workshops and continuing education.

Skills and Expertise – List the most **professionally relevant** skills you wish to use and be known for using. Look at your role models for ideas.

Endorsements – Begin gathering endorsements for those skills. The reciprocity principle works great here. Be liberal giving endorsements and others will respond in kind.

Volunteer Experience and Causes – Add any **professionally relevant** volunteer work. You may include anything that positions you as someone who is committed to contributing and adding value.

Additional Information

Interests - Add any **professionally relevant hobbies.** You may add other things that make you "interesting" but be careful with that.

Personal Details - Add any **professionally relevant** details including things that may help you appear stable or culturally in sync.

Honors & Awards - Add any **professionally relevant** awards. You might wish to include older business awards or even school awards that are not so relevant. This can position you as an achiever and someone who adds value and contributes wherever they go.

Organizations - Include any **professionally relevant** organizations. If you don't have any to include here…. **JOIN SOME!!!**

Recommendations – Shoot for 5 per year. The best way is to begin writing really good recommendations for others and they will reciprocate. In some cases you may also need to ask.

Connections – Set aside about 15 minutes a week to send connection invitations to colleagues in your industry.

Groups – Join 50 groups in your industry as fast as you can.

Following – Track people that you admire in your industry.

News – Follow industry information.

Companies – Follow companies and organizations that you might be interested in working for.

Schools – Follow any college you have attended.

Note: *LinkedIn* occasionally adds and removes profile components. These elements were current at the time of writing.

Congruence!!!

Make sure the information on your resume and application match the *LinkedIn* profile!!! Pay careful attention to employment dates… This will be checked.

Answers from page 126

Michael Jackson - Invented the "Moon Walk"

Neil Armstrong - First person to walk on the real moon

Lindsay Lohan - Actress in and out of rehab… and jail

Howard Stern - Shock Jock on the radio

Simon Cowell - Rude original judge on American Idol

Jacques Cousteau - Under the sea documentary film maker

The Kardashians - Spoiled sisters who are famous for being famous

Jim Henson - Creator of The Muppets

DREAM JOB!!!

"Generally, you have a quick entrance into the job market and enjoy a faster than traditional hiring process; ability to audition on a job for several weeks or months and get a foot inside a company where access might be difficult, if not impossible."

~Cathy A. Reilly, Author of *The Temp Factor*

Chapter 8
Staffing and Search Firms

If you are unwillingly to make direct contacts on potential employers, you should **not walk, but <u>run</u>** to every staffing service office within 25 miles of your home. Staffing services used to be referred to as temporary personnel agencies. In the past, they provided organizations with temporary workers for short-term assignments. In today's world these agencies do preliminary screening for long-term and permanent assignments. It's the primary way you can get an interview in many companies who are not set up to efficiently hire large numbers of employees.

Sign Up! The Value a Staffing Service

Your favorite actor has a talent agent and so does your favorite athlete. Maybe you should too! Staffing services can add a lot of value to candidates looking for full-time permanent work.

Consider what a staffing service offers:

1. Online application practice
2. Resume evaluation
3. Applicant tracking preparation
4. Interview practice
5. Feedback on appropriate attire

6. Assessment practice

7. Temp-to-Hire

8. Foot-in-the-Door (some companies only hire thru services)

9. Access to part of the "Hidden Job Market"

10. Free education and experience

11. Avoid a 6-month unemployment label

12. Overcome a 6-month unemployment label

13. Part-time work, leaving time for optimal job search

Consider these facts:

• 17,000 firms operate 35,000 agency offices in the U.S.

• 2.91 million are employed through services every day

• 11.5 million are employed through services each year

• 79% work full-time

• 75% of all staffing is temp-to-hire or temp-to-perm

• Each year, about 12 million people find work through staffing agencies

Approaching A Staffing Service

Here are some tips:

• Develop a relationship with your placement person

• Approach visits and interviews with a Stand Out mindset

• Bring a great resume and dress for an interview

• Be upfront about your goals

• Do not exaggerate your qualifications

• Accept assignments even if they aren't perfect

• Establish yourself as reliable and get to the top of the call list

• Follow up after the visit or interview

• Check in regularly to show interest

• Offer feedback after each assignment

Extend the same level of respect to a staffing service that you would to a valued employer!

Top National Staffing Companies:

Adecco Staffing

Aerotek

   Tek Systems

Apple One

Express Employment Professionals

Interim Healthcare

Kelly Services

   Kelly IT

Manpower

Robert Half

   Accountemps

   OfficeTeam

   The Creative Group

   Robert Half Technology

Spherion

Volt Workforce Solutions

America's Job Center

America's Job Center is a "One-Stop" access to employment related services. It is a bridge between candidates and employers. Each participating agency contributes what it does best, connecting organizations with those looking for work. Employers can get help in posting job openings and recruiting candidates. Job seekers can get assistance in assessing skills, finding job opportunities and training, prepping a resume and much more..

Job Search Strategy Training and Tools

Many job candidates lack the strategies and tools to conduct an effective job search. *America's Job Center* offers:

Job Search Planning Tools

Strengths Assessment Tools

Job Search Targeting Resources and Assistance

Resume Crafting Including Cover Letters and Reference Sheets

Interview Preparation

Visibility Contacts Into The Hidden Job Market

Employer Posting Resources

Relationship Networking Strategies

Job Search Office

Most job candidates do not have a home environment that is conducive to an effective job search. *America's Job Center* solves that problem by offering:

Free Desk Space

Free Computer Use

Free Microsoft Office Programs

Help and Support

Federal Government Training Assistance

On the Job Training (OJT), provides training in many different fields for people who are looking for permanent employment. Employers are reimbursed a percentage of the wages to offset the cost of training you on-the-job. Available jobs include entry-level positions. They also include help with the transfer of skills from one profession to another. For a location near you, conduct a *Google* search for *America's Job Center*.

Note: *America's Job Centers* are a terrific resource. They are independently managed and some locations are better than others. If you're not happy with one center, try another.

"Many people think I can't live a normal life because I don't have arms or legs. I could choose to believe that and give up trying. I could stay at home and wait for others to take care of me. Instead, I choose to believe that I can do anything, and I always try to do things my own way."

~Nick Vujicic, Author of *Life Without Limits*

Chapter 9
Search Challenges

This chapter includes a list of job search barriers, roadblocks, detours and ditches. Each of them can be very real. In some cases, for some people, they are either imaginary or magnified beyond what is real. But racism, sexism, ageism, schoolism and many more still exist in this country and every country. I don't want to minimize them. I also don't want you to magnify any one of them. Refuse to become a victim. If you are a victim, refuse to have a victim mentality. It's easy to believe that your problem is unusual or worse than what is common. I promise that with a little research, you can find a case that is much worse than what you're experiencing. And I promise you can find a person handling it with grit and grace. Be that person!

Disabilities

Many of the so-called disabilities or limitations are constraints that can be a source of focus. Like Da Vinci's drawing with the *"Vitruvian Man"* ideal, the hypothetical *"Vitruvian Brain"* ideal is in rapid decline. Let's look at a few of the more common disabilities and some people who have either overcome them and in many cases even leveraged them in positive ways.

Dyslexia

A disproportionate number of high level corporate CEO's and entrepreneurs have learning disabilities, including dyslexia. It could be argued this so-called "disability" provided them with some advantage. Consider this list of achievers widely believed to be dyslexic:

Charles Schwab - Founder, Discount Brokerage Business

Craig McCaw - Cellular Phone Pioneer

John Reed - Led *Citibank* to the top of the industry

Scott Adams - *Dilbert* Creator

James Carville - Political Consultant

Cher - Singer, Entertainer

Charles "Pete" Conrad Jr. - Astronaut

Erin Brockovich - Activist

Whoopi Goldberg - Actress, Talk Show Host

Dr. Edward Hallowell - Psychiatrist

Bill Hewlett - Co-founder, *Hewlett Packard*

Jay Leno - Host of *The Tonight Show*

Nelson Rockefeller - Former Governor of New York

Nolan Ryan - Hall of Fame Baseball Pitcher

Steven Spielberg - Film Maker

Thomas J. Watson Jr. - Former CEO, *IBM*

Henry Winkler - Actor

ADHD - Attention Deficit Hyperactivity Disorder

This is classified as a developmental disability characterized by attention and hyperactivity problems. But Lara Honos-Webb, an expert on ADHD and author of *The Gift of ADHD* writes, "Children with ADHD who have been labeled as spacy often have the capacity to solve problems created by rigid models of thinking. Daydreaming is the fount of creativity in that it is essentially the process of engaging the imagination…. Thomas Alva

Edison, who invented the light bulb and about a thousand other things, was characterized by an easy distractibility. He was known to have forty different inventions in progress at one time. He would work on one until he got bored with it and move on to another one as inspiration hit. Another word for distractibility is 'flexibility,' and it can be put to use in groundbreaking innovation and productivity."

Not only would Thomas Edison have been diagnosed with ADHD, it's likely that Albert Einstein would have been as well. If you've flown on *Jet Blue Airways*, you're already aware they are consistently rated as one of the top airlines in the world. Founder and CEO David Neeleman has been diagnosed with adult ADHD. He surrounds himself with people that compliment his strengths and fill in the weakness gaps.

Paul Orfalea is the founder of *Kinko's*, now known as *FedEx Office*. Orfalea believes his ADHD helped him build the business. As he describes it, he has the tendency to wander and so never spent much time in his office. He was always going from store to store. It was that wandering that allowed him to discover all the ideas that allowed him to expand his business.

Autism Spectrum

Typically characterized by social deficits, communication difficulties, stereotyped or repetitive behaviors and interests, and in some cases, cognitive delays, this disorder also offers potential gifts.

Evidence is increasing that Autism is common among Techies. People with this disorder master detail and tend to think in pictures much better than the general population. Bram Cohen has Asperger Syndrome, a form of Autism. Bram also writes software programs and in 2001 introduced *Bit Torrent*, described by *Business Week* as an ingenious, disruptive, and controversial piece of technology that is available for free and lets people easily exchange huge amounts of digital information.

Autistic children can grow up to do great things in the lower tech world as well. Stephen Shore's parents were told their son had Autism when he was only a toddler. After losing speech and withdrawing, symptoms that formerly led to being institutionalized, Stephen's parents decided to do the best they could with their son at home. They encouraged him, played music, helped him build a seashell collection, supported an interest in astronomy and kept him supplied with plenty of reading. Today he has two doctorates, has written two books and oversees an educational consulting company.

Mood Disabilities

I want to be especially careful with this one because depression can be seriously debilitating. Not only is quality of life and suicide a concern, but people who repeatedly experience depression often die early. Still, many high achievers suffered from serious bouts of mood disorder and one could argue that it helped shape their many positive qualities. Its link to creativity is fairly well established and in one study over 50% of writers and artists were confirmed as sufferers.

Abraham Lincoln suffered from bouts of depression. The 16th President experienced a lot of setbacks and outright tragedy. Whether or not his bouts with mood were solely as a result of circumstances, a result of a brain chemical imbalance or a combination of both, we may never know. Regardless, he was one of this country's deepest and greatest thinkers.

British Prime Minister and leader of *World War II* era England, Winston Churchill unabashedly spoke of what he called his black dog. What he described as a lifelong battle with depression didn't seem to mute his significant achievements. Churchill was a gifted painter, writer, politician, as well as wartime commander and chief. It's hard to imagine him finding time for depression but it characterized much of his life.

In May of 2012, Edvard Munch's famous painting, *The Scream* sold for 119.2 million dollars. It was, at the time, a new world record price for art. It is said Munch somehow channeled his mood into the painting.

Anxiety Disabilities

Characterized by excessive watchfulness and avoidance behaviors, some believe that anxiety is as important to the creative process as mood. This thinking is bolstered by those numbered in the performing arts who suffer. A short list includes Roseanne Barr, David Bowie, Cher, Donny Osmond, Johnny Depp, Sheryl Crow, Aretha Franklin and Ray Charles. Barbara Streisand's anxiety has kept her off stage for the better part of several decades. Woody Allen says he makes movies to combat anxiety.

Although I grew weary of *Oakland Raider* owner Al Davis' antics and eventually switched to the team across the bay, I loved the *Raiders* when coached by John Madden. Most football fans are aware of Madden's fear of flying. His crisscrossing of the country every year, in the now legendary "Madden Cruiser", allows him to deliver his color commentary on each week's top football game. The custom motor home is part of his persona. You could argue whether or not this anxiety has actually made him more popular, but at the least it seems to have been managed in a way that hasn't suppressed his success in any way.

Down Syndrome

Intellectual disabilities may carry some of the greatest stigmas with regard to how they might impede our cultural ideas of success. But I have to tell you, one of the most emotionally powerful and uplifting funerals I have ever attended was for Benny. Person after person stood up at this funeral to tell about the positive impact Benny had on their life. Benny held down a real job and was a valued volunteer in his church.

How many parents have had to endure these harsh words of an insensitive doctor? "Your child will be mentally retarded. He'll never sit or stand, walk or talk. He'll never be able to distinguish you from any other adults. He'll never read or write or have a single meaningful thought or idea. The common practice for these children is to place them in an institution immediately."

Emily and Charles Pearl heard these words and this particular doctor went on to add, "Go home and tell your friends and family that he died in childbirth." Fortunately, Emily and Charles didn't listen to that doctor. By age 19, their Down syndrome son Jason, had become an actor in the television show *The Fall Guy.* He had also co-authored a book titled *Count Me In* where he offers some thoughts about what he might share with that doctor who had so negatively counseled his parents. Jason stated, "People with disabilities can learn! Like learning languages, going to other foreign nations, going to teen groups and teen parties, going to cast parties, becoming independent, being a lighting board operator, an actor, the backstage crew. I would talk about history, math, English, algebra, business math, global studies. I will tell him that I play the violin, that I make relationships with other people, I make oil paintings, I play the piano, I can sing, I am competing in sports, in the drama group, that I have many friends and I have a full life."

In recent years, individuals with Down syndrome have even moved beyond working in sheltered workshops, supportive environments and regular jobs without support. Today we see some of them moving into entrepreneurial roles. Clara Link travels all over the country as a photographer. Ruth Tonack is a water color artist and Sujeet Desai is a musician.

Schizophrenia

Of all the conditions I've discussed, Schizophrenia remains one of the most shrouded in mystery. Although it has multiple forms and manifestations, I recommend the movie *A Beautiful Mind* to get a quick picture. It portrays the life of John Nash, an American mathematician who won the 1994 *Nobel Prize* in Economics.

In spite of unusual thoughts, perceptions, delusions and hallucinations, some with this condition manage a productive life. If you haven't rocked out at a *Beach Boys* concert you haven't lived a full life. Yet band leader and chief song writer Brian Wilson lives with this condition. So does acclaimed artist Salvador Dali, fiction writer Philip K. Dick, *Broadway* star Meera Popkin and Russian dancer Vaclav Nijinsky.

Again, it's not my purpose to place rose colored glasses on anyone. What the people with any of these conditions go through is at best extraordinarily difficult. It is extremely hard for their families as well. What I do hope to convey, is that their lives are still valuable. And keeping with the theme of this book, they have amazing talents, strengths and gifts. They have unique contributive advantages to offer in spite of the conditions they face, and in some cases because of the conditions they face.

Note: I am not a mental health professional and I don't claim a high level of expertise on these conditions. My purpose is to give hope and inspiration to the individuals who face these conditions as well as their families.

Most of the material in this chapter was pulled from three resources:

The Power of Neurodiversity by Thomas Armstrong PhD
The Gift of Dyslexia by Ronald D. Davis with Eldon M. Braun
The Gift of ADHD by Lara Honos-Webb
Article-*The Dyslexic CEO: Charles Schwab, Richard Branson, Craig McCaw, & John Chambers Triumphed over America's No. 1 Learning Disorder and Your Kids Can Too*, Betsy Morris in *Fortune Magazine*, May 2002

Nick Vujicic was born with no arms and no legs. He lives an amazing life as an author and motivational speaker. Chef Jeff Henderson discovered his passion and gift for cooking while serving time in prison for dealing drugs. Today he uses his position as a Celebrity Chef to help others transform their lives and live their dreams. Head for their websites and be inspired!

http://www.nickvujicic.com
http://chefjefflive.com

In their book *Job-Hunting for the So-Called Handicapped*, Richard Bolles and Dale Susan Brown offer an interesting hypothetical that I've adapted for this book:

Imagine the human race had an Abilities Bank, in which there were a total of 13,000 Abilities and each one of us at birth had to go to that bank and choose 700 that we would use for the rest of our life here on earth. You and I, of course, would not choose the same 700. You might choose to be good at analyzing things, while I might choose to be good at drawing. The varying abilities we chose would make us different from one another, even unique.

But how would you describe yourself after this choosing of abilities? Would you point out those abilities you have and the tasks you can do well? If so, you would be emphasizing your abilities. Or would you point out the 12,300 things that you still can't do – even if some other members of the human race can? If so, you would be emphasizing your DIS-abilities.

Bolles and Brown suggest that everyone has DIS-abilities or things we can't do. Every one is enabled and everyone is disabled. Everyone is CAPable and everyone is handiCAPped. Each and every human has both sides. That's the nature of the life that is given to us all.

Go through the following list and put a check mark next to anything that might apply to you. If you are struggling with it, go get some assistance. There are people and organizations who want to help. Start with *America's Job Center* listed at the end of the last chapter. Ask for a referral.

Addiction
Recovering from chemical addiction
In treatment program
Non-recovering

Address
None

Age
Older
Young

Appearance
Body Language
Incomplete Wardrobe (no belt or socks)
Messy
Disfigurement
Hair Style
Hair Cut/Length
Hygiene
Dental
Demeanor – How I land or come across to people
Presentation
Tattoos Exposed
Piercings, Gauges

Application Forms
Incomplete – leaving blanks and not complying with requests
Messy
No English
Poor Spelling
Lack Selling Points

Attitude
Anger
Lack Initiative/Ambition
Negativity
Rudeness
Unprofessional
Unwillingness to Learn/Change/Adapt
Shyness
Low Self Esteem
Gruffness

Accessibility
No Phone
No Voicemail
No Cell Phone Voice Mail Set Up
No Professional Email
Message Service Issues
Shared Voicemail

Business Culture
Lack of Knowledge
Fears
Inappropriate

Character Choices
Dishonesty
Not Showing Up For Work
Punctuality – Not Showing Up On Time
Dependability

Childcare
Lack Babysitter
Pregnancy
Special Needs Child
Child Illness
Single Parent

Communication
Limited English
No English
Not Bilingual
Limited Vocabulary
Profanity, Vulgarity
Speech Impediment
Strong Accent
Slang
Poor Grammar

Computer Literacy
Keyboard Knowledge
Keyboard Speed
Keyboard Accuracy
Software
Microsoft Office Skills
Hardware
Operating Systems – *Windows, Mac*

Disability
Emotional
Learning
Mental
Physical

Domestic Violence
Domestic Violence – New Identity
Domestic Violence – Self Esteem

Education
Lack GED
Lack Specific Knowledge
No Degree
Wrong Degree

Employer Bias Concern/Fear
Gender
Race
Religion
LGBTQ

Environment/Relationships
Non-Supportive
Lack of Tools/Resources

Fear
Fear of Failure
Fear of Rejection
Fear of Responsibility
First Job

Financial
Credit Score
Leans

Gang Member
Gang Member – Former
Gang Member – Active
Gang Member - Appearance

Grief-Loss
Death of Loved One
Divorce
Job Loss

Health
Chronic Illness
Physical Disability
Teeth
Overweight
Underweight
Mental Illness
Too Many Sick Days
Smoking

Housing
Homeless Current
Homeless Former
Unstable – Living With Friends
Unstable – Living in Shelter

Identification
Green Card
No Driver's License
No *Social Security* Card

Illiteracy
Low Reading Skills
No Reading Skills

Immigration
Immigrant – Legal
Immigrant - Illegal

Job Search
Lack Resources
Lack Skills
Lack Current Knowledge
Inability to Market Self – Talent Issue
Won't Market Self – Pride Issue
Resume Ineffective
Poor Interview Skills
Unaware of Strengths, Talents, Passion, Values, Knowledge, Skills, Personality

Ineffective at Describing/Demonstrating Strengths
Lack Professional References
Lack Professional Resume
Lack Applicant Tracking System Compatible Resume
Lack Cover Letter
Lack Interview Skills
Lack Professional Portfolio
Lack Professional Associates in Target Career
Lack Professional Associates
Lack *LinkedIn* Profile

Language
Poor English
Poor Spelling
Poor Grammar

Legal
Probation
Restrictive Probation
Community Service
Traffic Violations – Driving Record
Protection from Violence
DUI
Criminal Record – Felony
Criminal Record - Misdemeanor
Megan's List

Local Job Market
Unemployment Rate
Company-Skill Match
Public Transportation

Location
Distance from Target Jobs
High Unemployment Rate
Health Issues

Medical Benefits
Need Health Insurance

Mental Health Conditions
Depression
Bipolar
Social Anxiety
Personality Disorders

Urgency
Need Job Now

Parents
Aging, Illness, Primary Caregiver

Safety
Violent Relationship

Skills
Hasn't Learned to Drive
Computer - Keyboarding
Software

Technology

Training
Lack Targeted Skills
Lack Specific Skills
Skills Out Of Date

Transportation
Lack Car
Lack Reliable Car
Lack Gas Money
Lack Driver's License or Suspended
Lack Car Insurance
Public Transportation

Trauma
Past Abuse
PTSD

Work History
Too Little Experience
Too Much Experience
Unrelated Experience
Laid Off
Fired
Gaps In Employment
Hopping – Short Periods of Employment
No Work History in United States
No Legal Work History
Self Employed Work History
Overqualified

Workman's Comp
Complaint Filed
Past Complaint Company on Resume/Work History

"Doing the best in this moment puts you in the best place for the next moment."

~Oprah Winfrey

Chapter 10
Job Shifting

In chapter 2, on Career Targets, I talked about the A-B-C-D formula for success:

Any Job
Better Job
Career Job
Dream Job

I want to flesh that out in this chapter with some examples. You must focus on giving your absolute best in every single role you find yourself in, even those that have very little connection to your dream. You must also have the courage to change roles and move toward your dream.

Comedian and television star Steve Harvey has written a brilliant book titled, *Act Like a Success – Think Like A Success*. Harvey talks about selecting the right vehicle for your unique strengths. He begins, "The people who are truly successful use the vehicle that is right for today to work toward the next upgrade that will lead to an even higher rung of success. You need to be open to connecting to a vehicle that connects to your current level. That means begin now where you are."

Harvey is spot on. I can't tell you how many people I work with who expect to begin at the top. School has prepared them to begin a new career and they want to cut into line ahead of those who have several years experience. They don't want to pay their dues. School gets you to the starting line, not the finish line.

Harvey talks about Beyonce's career, how she started off as a child singer and the road she took to become a stadium filler. Beyonce started off in a group called *Girls Tyme*. That group lost a competition to a boy band no one ever heard of again. But *Girls Tyme* was the first of many vehicles Beyonce used to climb to the top. *Destiny's Child* was another. Tours and albums included *Sasha Fierce* and then *Mrs. Carter*.

Harvey says, "Beyonce always used the vehicle that was available to her at the moment to work toward the next opportunity of her lifetime." He continues, "You do not have to bog down your journey trying to find a vehicle that will get you all the way to your final destination. The first vehicle that you attach yourself to may not be the one that finishes your journey. Simply attach yourself to a vehicle that gets your gift into motion."

The Transfer

I love Harvey's analogy of the bus transfer. "Think about this in terms of traveling on a city bus from one location to the next. Often you have to get a transfer in order to complete the journey. You will then be led to another transfer, which will take you to your second vehicle." The same analogy works if you are more familiar with air travel. We all want non-stop destination flights sitting in first class with someone bringing us drinks. But none of us start there.

Harvey then moves on to tell about his own career transfers. He worked very hard physical jobs until he was inspired by an old friend (Arsenio Hall) to take his shot in comedy at age 30.

Look at Harvey's career path and the transfers:

Amateur Night – Working for **Free**
Paid Gigs - $25.00 a Night
Featuring Act - $350.00 per Week
Featuring Act II - $750.00 per Week
Small Club National Headliner - $1500.00 per Week
Large Club National Headliner - $60,000 per Week
Large Club - $25,000 per Night

Consider that in order to go forward, you may have to go backward for a short period. Notice that Steve Harvey started out working for free and then for a non-livable wage. You may have to take an unpaid internship and work for minimum wage for a few months before you begin your climb.

Harvey asks a great question, "Are you so busy looking for the luxury vehicle now, that your level of development can't afford it?"

In my own case, I started teaching strengths in a church setting, for free. At one point the pastor asked me to meet with each of the staff and discuss their strengths and how they connected with their ministry role. There was no pay for this. I helped start a job search program and taught the strengths part of the process each week, again for free. After two years of that, I finally got a paying gig, working at a career college.

Bloom where you are planted!!! But be willing to re-pot yourself every few years. Make sure your soil has all the best nutrients. Keep growing.

People who are successful have big dreams but they are willing to start very small. Identify a big target or dream job and then backward map it. And it's okay to change dreams as you get closer. Sometimes dreams look different up close. But get started!

"You will re-write your job description under the nose of your boss, and they will love you for it."

~Marcus Buckingham

Chapter 11
Job Shaping

In this chapter, I want to introduce you to strategies that will help you shift your existing job toward your strengths. You're going to find a job, a career and if you're diligent, you'll get your dream job. But none of these jobs, even your dream job, will fit perfectly at first. Like a good suit of clothes, you'll have to tailor it.

Job crafting has been encouraged since the 1930's and 1940's but the concept really took off when Amy Wrzesniewski and Jane Dutton began sharing about workplace research at a midwestern hospital in the year 2000. Both were working at the *University of Michigan's Ross School of Business* when they interviewed members of a hospital janitorial staff. They asked questions about the janitor's work experience, the activities they enjoyed and parts of the job they found lacking. What Wrzesniewski and Dutton discovered, both stunned and inspired.

The interviews revealed two types of workers. The first group experienced their job just as you might imagine a hospital cleaning staff would. They didn't find their work especially satisfying. They didn't describe it as being highly skilled. And when they described their workplace activities, they generally recited the job description. When the researchers inquired about the workers' motivation, "benefits" was the most common response.

The second group was completely different. They enjoyed the work. They found it quite meaningful. They saw the work they did everyday as being very highly skilled. And when Wrzesniewski and Dutton asked about tasks and relationships at work, they described their experiences quite differently than the first group.

This second group described cleaning rooms and paying careful attention to emotionally struggling patients as rewarding. They would often double back and spend time with the patients, have conversations and give them opportunities to cry. At discharge, they sometimes walked patients through the confusing corridor maze all the way to their cars. This last activity was actually an offense for which they could have been fired.

One of the janitors, who worked in the coma recovery wing, on her own initiative, regularly rotated the wall hangings and moved pictures around between rooms. Her rationale was that by changing the environment, it might somehow spark recovery in those patients. When asked about whether this was part of her job description, she responded, "That's not part of my job... but that's part of me."

After doing further follow up with leadership, the researchers discovered there was a whole group of workers engaging with their work in a completely different way. The hospital management had no idea this was going on. The workers were often breaking rules and operating completely outside the bounds of their job descriptions. The team dug deeper to see if there were variances in the work teams, the shifts or management oversight. They found absolutely no difference.

In subsequent research, Wrzesniewski and Dutton found this type of phenomenon going on in all types of organizations around the country. The name they gave this role reconstruction activity was "Job Crafting".

In an interview with *Bloomberg's Business Week*, Wrzesniewski, now at the *Yale School of Management*, says she defines job crafting as "**a naturally occurring phenomenon in which employees treat their jobs as a collection of tasks that can be molded and reorganized to fit their individual strengths, passions, and motives**." According to Wrzesniewski, "The accountant who makes his job less repetitive by creating a new method for filing taxes and the engineer who acquires more social contact by regularly offering to help her team members are both crafting their jobs."

As the research grew and became more specific, the team found this job crafting took at least 3 different forms:

Task Crafting – Individuals alter the number, nature or type of tasks they do. The staff member who rotated the hospital room pictures around is an example of this.

Relationship Crafting – Individuals redesign the nature of the relationships and interactions in ways that change how they think about the meaning of their work. An example might be, taking the initiative to forge relationships with team members across functions in ways that increase value to clients and the organization.

Cognitive Crafting – Individuals modify the perception of the tasks and their meaning. Sometimes this meant actually changing their job title. When asked about what role they played at the hospital, the first group of workers simply told the researchers they were janitors. But in the second group, they described their role using terms like, "Hospital Ambassador" or "Healer". When asked about the "Healer" role, one worker responded, "I create sterile spaces in which patients heal. I do everything I can to facilitate their healing whether it's caring for the patients' families or coordinating with their nurses." Wrzesniewski maintains, "None of this is just a trick of the mind. It actually influences how, when, where and with whom the work is done. The job descriptions were changed pretty radically."

And again, Wrzesniewski and Dutton's research has shown that all three types of job crafting is happening in every industry and every level of the organization, top to bottom. It's going on in organizations where workers are expected to craft their jobs and even in organizations where people are explicitly forbidden.

If you're a person who feels a strong need to control your employees or are just concerned about hospital safety, you may have concerns about this story. For some, the idea of allowing employees to decide what they want to be called is madness. I've worked in organizations that seemed to spend an inordinate amount of time deciding on job titles. In the 1980's, Tom Peters shared numerous stories about progressive organizations who gave their employees freedom to decide what they would be called. My favorite was the story of Sarah Clifton, a line worker at the hugely successful *W.L. Gore* corporation. Sarah's business card title read, "Supreme Commander".

Wrzesniewski's research has subsequently focused on the business impact that flows out of an employee's freedom to craft their job. She shares several positive outcomes. Job crafting is associated with increases in job satisfaction, commitment, organizational loyalty, performance increases and mobility to new roles.

Finally, Wrzesniewski offers a few suggestions for implementing job crafting at the organizational, team or business unit level. The first suggestion is explicitly offering increased autonomy for means and methods of attaining organizational results. Second, build job crafting discussions into performance evaluations, asking employees about changes they would like to make to the job that are still aligned with the organization's mission. Third, allowing employees to share or trade tasks, moving toward the goal of getting everyone in the organization doing what they do best. One person's dread is another person's delight.

If you'd like to watch a short 12 minute talk that Amy Wrzesniewski gave at *Google's Re:Work* seminar, go to *Job Crafting - Amy Wrzesniewski on "Creating Meaning in Your Own Work" YouTube*. It covers most of what I've discussed in this post. I highly recommend their *Job Crafting Exercise* booklet you can pick up at www.jobcrafting.com.

Here are four more ways you can begin shaping an existing job. The first strategy is to simply become aware that successful people operate very differently. As an example, we'll look at two specific roles, Supreme Court Justices and Military Generals.

The second strategy is a way to make your day progressively more strengths oriented. I call it *STRENGTHSPATH* Math.

The third strategy is retiring your weaknesses.

Lastly, I will summarize with a grouping of seven options to consider when you find yourself in work that doesn't fit.

Strategy One: Awareness of Unique Approaches

We have nine Supreme Court Justices. Each Justice does the same job, although the Chief Justice may have some oversight responsibilities. Political leanings, philosophy, values and beliefs aside, they all approach their jobs quite differently. There is a wide range of style, personality and temperament among the nine justices.

Anthony Kennedy leans forward to ask questions. Often these questions display feelings and take an emotional tone. But rarely do these expressions give away how he will actually vote.

Justice **Samuel Alito** also asks questions. They often cut straight to the heart of the issue the court is hearing. But unlike Kennedy, his questions often give away his thoughts, feelings and how he will likely vote.

Stephen Breyer is known for his complex hypothetical questions. Some have ranked him as the most talkative Justice on the Court.

Justice **Clarence Thomas** is the least talkative and rarely asks a question. He went over 6 years without making a single inquiry. In a 2009 *C-Span* interview Thomas said, "I think there are far too many questions. Some members of the court like that interaction. I prefer to listen and think it through more quietly."

The three women Justices, **Ruth Bader Ginsburg, Sonia Sotomayor** and **Elena Kagan** are completely different. They often jockey to be the first to ask a question. They sometimes interrupt a lawyer's initial presentation in the first few syllables. And often these questions are sharply worded. Ginsburg's questions come out slowly and clearly enunciated. Kagan tends to ask big picture analytical questions. Sotomayor can be demanding of lawyers and is not afraid to butt heads with other Justices.

Anthony Scalia (recently deceased) was the funniest and most likely to bring laughter into the courtroom. Next to Breyer, Scalia was ranked as the second most talkative. Scalia replacement **Neil Gorsuch** is very early in his tenure as I write this. Some observers have suggested he is not shy or cautious and might be a cross between Scalia and Kagan.

As the Chief Justice, **John Roberts** reins in the lawyers and, at times, his fellow Justices. He usually saves his questions for last.

What about World War II generals like **Eisenhower, Bradley, Patton and MacArthur**? Surely they were similar in talent and temperament. Not so.

Eisenhower was a talented administrator. He was a people person and a gifted diplomat. Temperamentally he was well-suited to keep all the allied generals fighting Germans and not each other. But he didn't have the battlefield talent of the other three. Eisenhower could also match Patton word for word with ferocious outbursts when the circumstances called for it.

MacArthur was a gifted administrator like Eisenhower but more of an egomaniac. His staff loved him but he was often in conflict with his peers.

Patton was a loose canon whose real genius was on the battlefield. He tended to not think before he spoke and, unlike Eisenhower, had no sense of the need to build coalitions with allies.

Bradley was a great team player who was an excellent planner and meticulous in his execution. The foundation of Bradley's success was a strong ability to grasp all the pieces on a huge moving battlefield.

The point of these examples is that there are a lot of ways to be successful at the same job. According to family therapist Virginia Satir, there are at least 250 ways to wash the dishes. In my work as a manager, I have observed sales people reach the pinnacle of success with quite different strengths and ways of going about their day to day work. This is possible with most jobs, including the job of running the country. In my book, *The STRENGTHSPATH PRINCIPLE*, I cover a few of the U.S. Presidents in some detail.

Strategy Two: *STRENGTHSPATH* Math

Try the mathematical approach to change. Every week identify one work activity that you either hate or aren't very good at. **SUBTRACT** that activity. Stop doing it. If the activity is essential, trade with someone. Hire someone. Find an intern. Outsource it. Then **ADD** one activity you love every week. Figure out what you love doing and then figure out how to integrate it with your current duties.

Stay with this adding and subtracting method until you've created your dream job.

A few readers should start looking for a new job immediately. Your job fits so poorly it's a mental health issue. I recently talked to a very gifted woman who had awards all over her wall for achievements at work. But she went home and cried herself to sleep every night. She quit and loves what she does now.

There are two kinds of total career makeovers, internal and external. With internal makeovers you make an effort to stay in the same company. With external makeovers you change companies.

Strategy Three: Progressively Retire Non-Talents

Dr. Robert Schuller, founder of the *Crystal Cathedral Congregation* in Garden Grove, California, is a hero of mine at so many levels. My Mom,

Dad, both sets of Grandparents and myself tuned into his weekly *Hour of Power* broadcasts. I still have my Dad's copy of Dr. Schuller's early book, *Move Ahead With Possibility Thinking*. His teaching and ministry got me through some of the most difficult times of my life. In one of Schuller's later books, *If It Is To Be, It's Up To Me,* he writes on the concept of progressive early retirement. Schuller begins:

"How do I find the time to manage a weekly world-wide television ministry? And write books? And build a strong and happy family based on a loving marriage that's close to a joyous fiftieth anniversary?

I learned early in life how and when to 'retire'. I've now passed the forty-year anniversary in my ministerial work. At the end of my first year on the job as pastor I began to 'retire'. I retired from the job of janitor, for example. I haven't cleaned floors or toilets since! And that retirement freed up time for other duties. At the end of my second year I retired from my job as secretary, no longer typing my own letters. I found time to do other worthwhile church work. At the end of my third year, I retired as business manager. I haven't deposited money or written a check for the parish since then. I was released to use my time more productively. At the end of my fourth year, I retired as a department leader and teacher. I found the church a better replacement, and I had more time to write. At the end of my fifth year, then sixth year – yes, every passing year – I retired from further time consuming duties. At the end of my tenth year I finally retired as marriage counselor. The counseling center was opened and staffed as part of our ministry, and I found a lot of time – time that was instantly filled with new ideas that needed top priority on my clock and calendar. At the end of my fifteenth year we launched the television ministry, and I retired as the senior minister managing the staff of a large local congregation. At the end of my twenty-fifth year I retired as my car driver. I can now read books, dictate letters, and read my mail – all from the back seat of a car. At the end of my fortieth year I retired from five days a week in the office to become a minister at large in the world, filling a role only my face and name could fill."

Schuller continues, " Learn how to retire selectively from those duties you've always done. Focus on the role where you're irreplaceable. You'll be surprised at how well, wisely and fruitfully your time will then be managed." He exhorts us later in the book with some advice on what might inform our retirement choices when he says, "Look for something you enjoy and are pretty good at, and go for it."

When should you start this early retirement program? I think age 8 works. The school system will object and you will still need to pitch in with family chores, but why not start early? Tiger Woods did and so did Warren Buffett.

Strategy Four: Finding Yourself in Work You Don't Enjoy

All of us will have some frog swallowing to do in life and at work. But if you find yourself swallowing frogs all day long, you need to make change. My advice: Don't quit your current job before you've received a written job offer that fits better. There are some exceptions but they are rare. But eventually…

"If it doesn't fit you have to quit."
~Unknown wise person

The late *Tonight Show* host, Johnny Carson advised, "Never continue in a job you don't enjoy. If you are happy in what you are doing, you will like yourself, you will have inner peace and if you have that, along with physical health, you will have more success than you could possibly have imagined." John Maxwell said, "You will never fulfill your destiny doing work you despise."

7 Ways to Change Jobs

There are at least seven ways to change jobs. You can experiment with four of the ways while staying in your current position. The fifth way may allow you to stay with the same company in a different role. Ideas six and seven are more dramatic moves, although each can often be accomplished in ways that reduce risk:

1. **Restructure Your Job** – Change the who, when, where, aspects of your work
2. **Reduce Your Job Tasks** – Specialize or reduce variety
3. **Expand Your Job Tasks** – Generalize or increase variety
4. **Change How You Do It** - Adjust your approach
5. **Change Jobs** – Task Sets – If you're in sales go into accounting
6. **Change Companies** – Align with an organization that matches your values
7. **Start a Business** – Take on some side work

I recommend *The 10% Entrepreneur* by Patrick McGinnis and *The Leap* by Rick Smith. They outline low-risk ways of getting started.

Many people are doing what they are designed to do, but only partially. Maybe you are in a situation where half of what you do fits very well but the other half doesn't. There isn't always a solution to this. But sometimes you can negotiate a restructuring of your position with your company. Sometimes you can get it accomplished "off the books" by trading activities.

Some workers would be much more effective if they were doing a very focused subset of their current responsibilities. They need to specialize. An individualized version of what Jack Welch did with *General Electric* would be perfect.

When Welch took over *G.E.* in 1981, it was a respectable company. But it was a very diverse company that included 350 different businesses. Welch believed *G.E.* could be even better. What was his strategy? He used the *STRENGTHSPATH Principle*. He Discovered what *G.E.* was best at, Developed those businesses, and then Delivered them in a very focused way out in the marketplace. In his own words,

Welch describes the process:

"To the hundreds of businesses and product lines that made up the company we applied a single criterion: can they be number 1 or number 2 at whatever they do in the world marketplace? Of the 348 businesses or product lines that could not, we closed some and divested others. Their sale brought in almost $10 billion. We invested $18 billion in the ones that remained and further strengthened them with $17 billion worth of acquisitions. What remained in 1989 were 14 world-class businesses, each one either first or second in the world market in which it participates."

Most workers could benefit from a personalized version of what *G.E.* did. Think about how you can close down some of the activities you aren't the best at. Sell off or outsource some others.

A few workers would be much more effective if they did just the opposite and expanded their duties. Some people are very gifted with broad categories of work and thrive on variety. They need to generalize.

"When the music changes, so does the dance."

~African Proverb

Chapter 12
Job Search Jazz

In this section, I want to draw a comparison between music, specifically jazz, and how you can maximize your job search. Jazz is unique for its improvisation, call and response communication, complex rhythms, optimal venue and its ability to incorporate nearly anything that happens. Each of these components can be symbolically related to job search. For those of you that love metaphor or even a poetic approach to job search, this might be helpful.

Improvisation

Jazz is a unique form of music because improvisation is a key component . Just as you won't experience two identical days, you will never hear the same jazz piece performed the same way twice. It would be recognizable as the same song but would be altered. Jazz is about feeling the audience, seeing how they respond, and adjusting your set and style. **Great job search should be improvisational as well.** It should fit the circumstances and the people involved, incorporating on-the-fly adjustments in the moment.

Old models of job search training were much more rigid. You were handed the score and expected to play it precisely. Today, job search is much more like jazz. I may follow a set flow and structure, but with plenty of room for improvisation depending on what is happening on each unique day.

With jazz you have to know and be able to perform the score with spot-on accuracy. Each note and phrase must be in place. And then you make it your own. This is true with strengths based job search. You've got to have your structure, sequence, phrases... what you do and when you do it, down cold. Don't walk into your daily gig and just play random notes and phrases. You've got to have a very clear idea of what you want to have happen. You need to know the impact you want to make at work.

The greatest improvisational performer of all-time is well known to the public for everything except his improvisation. Even when sitting in with other musicians he couldn't resist changing their compositions on the fly. The improviser was Johann Sebastian Bach. **In the 18th century, improvisation was regarded as an integral component of serious music**. Bach and other composers of the time rarely spelled out parts for each instrument. They were expected to riff. When notes were specified on the sheet, musicians routinely threw in improvised flourishes. Like my wife Susy, who when cooking, sprinkles an extra dash of this and sprig of that.

Bach was famous for the extent of his improvisational boldness. He would embellish on the organ even in the middle of church services. In other performances, he would take musical themes tossed at him from the audience and immediately improvise around them, something more like a nightclub comic. Bach participated in improvisational duels with other musicians. And so it should be, as you play out each of your days.

Call and Response

Great job search is a conversation, not a monologue. Many people just walk through their day oblivious to those around them. The best at job search, engage their day in dialogue. They ask for and wait for a response, holding the white spaces or silence until a partner steps up and grabs the microphone, owning his or her part.

The complexities of jazz, display call and response in many forms. It can be a dialogue between the pianists left hand and right hand, an exchange of the instrumentalist and vocalist or between a soloist and a choir. True jazz is always a conversation between the performers and the audience. A partnership is formed. The circle moves wider to include dancing of all kinds from free style to friendly games of leapfrog. It includes non-dancers too. Their focused attention and foot tapping become part of the performance. And so it is with job search. Is dancing, leapfrog or at least some toe tapping part of your day? Great job search is a made up, spontaneous, collaborative conversation with potential employers, potential colleagues and co-workers.

Daily Rhythm

Rhythm is everywhere in nature. The ebb and flow of the sea that Susy and I walk beside each day has a rhythm. There is the same rhythm each day, yet each day has subtle shifts.

There is a polyrhythmic quality to jazz that often follows an impulse to simultaneously play 4/4 alongside 3/4 and 6/8. Rhythm is also inextricably tied to pace. The rhythm seems to drive the music along in time, so much so, that it is often referred to as "keeping time". In one sense it creates time.

Every day has a pace and rhythm. Each has an optimal tempo that should be governed by the content, amount of information, and tools used. The pace should also be drawn from the emotional intent of each part of the day. Pay attention to the mood you want to create at any given point. This can include excitement, peace, laughter or suspense. But mostly, the pace and rhythm of a day needs to be informed by the intrinsic tempo of the individual activity. In the case of simultaneous multiple activities, there is a collective cadence that you want to discover and at least initially match.

I have made sales presentations with small children in the room. Not only were they not interested in my content, they were on a completely different pace than what was optimal for the presentation. I learned to keep a small set of crayons and some pages to color on with me in my briefcase at all times. I did everything I could to set them up with their own rhythm while I worked on a completely different one with their parents.

Selection and Creation of Venue

Every style of music has a venue type that is better suited for the style. Rock is big music that seems to work best in big venues like outdoor stadiums and huge indoor arenas. Classical works well in concert halls created for that type of music. To me, jazz works best in a more intimate "club" kind of environment. When I've experienced rock n roll in a small club, I seem to walk away with a headache. When a jazz ensemble advances in popularity to the point where they fill a huge venue, it seems like they lose something to the environment. It just doesn't work as well.

Beyond size, there are many other dimensions of environment that either enhance or detract from a performance. Everything possible should be considered to insure all the ingredients are working together to create an optimal outcome. Lighting, seating, color, texture, sound system, acoustics, and staging are only the beginning of considerations. What does the musician want the audience to feel or do? When they sell a song or a musical number, they are looking toward a particular response. The audience attends because they want to respond. What is that response? Toe tapping, clapping, dancing, singing along? Maybe the musician even wants the people to participate by purchasing a recording or t-shirt. In this case music becomes sales. Does the musician want everyone to return and pay to hear him play again? … More sales! Think through everything.

Your job search is no different. Venue selection and creation can make or break you. Pay attention to detail. Control what you can control. What size room is optimal? What are the acoustics? What are the seating arrangements? How many chairs are needed? Who should sit where? What about climate control? It's difficult to communicate, let alone sell, teach or inform, if people are too hot or too cold. Sometimes you have to play in the room you are given. But you can often get permission to create minor last minute adjustments that can make a huge difference.

Think of all the venues you play in during the day. Your office, *Starbucks*, *America's Job Center*, your car, where you stop for lunch or breaks, where you meet your employees or prospective customers are all possibilities. Make sure your venues are well staged and orchestrated to set you up for success. Think about your instruments, song selection and set length.

Use Everything

There is a certain flexibility in jazz that allows the great musician to incorporate whatever happens to show up into a piece. Jazz great, and keyboard artist, Herbie Hancock played with the *Miles Davis Band*. Miles is on the short list of the greatest jazz musicians of all time. In Herbie's inspirational musical documentary, *Possibilities,* he said, "Miles could use anything." He went on to explain, "Whatever another performer did, whatever showed up, Miles could masterfully work it into the piece and do it on the fly." Learn to use everything that shows up in a day. That's great job search strategy.

"At its root, Scrum is based on a simple idea: whenever you start a project, why not regularly check in, see if what you're doing is heading in the right direction. And question whether there are any ways to improve how you're doing what you're doing, any ways of doing it better and faster, and what might be keeping you from doing that."

~Jeff Sutherland

Chapter 13
Agile Project Management
Job Search

Agile platforms are project management frameworks originated at *Toyota*, and are now being implemented by thousands of individuals, teams and organizations in all types of industries all over the world. In 1986, it took *General Motors* 40 hours to manufacture a car with an average of 13 defects per car. In the same year, *Toyota* could manufacture an equal car in 18 hours with 4.5 defects. What allowed *Toyota* to outperform *General Motors* at this level? There was only one significant difference. *Toyota* had been using an *Agile* project management framework known as *Lean*. In recent years, *General Motors* has used *Lean* to completely close that gap.

Building contractors now use *Agile* as do farmers, classroom teachers and wedding planners. *National Public Radio Teams* began using *Agile* strategies during the chaotic events of the Arab Spring. It has spread throughout the organization and then to teams at the *Washington Post*, *New York Times* and *Chicago Tribune*. The *Grameen Foundation* is using *Agile* methodologies to eliminate poverty in Uganda.

Agile has diversified into multiple frameworks including *Extreme Programing*, *Kanban*, and *Scrum*. You can transform your job search using the same project management framework that the world's top companies are using to build products and services.

There are several benefits of the *Agile* framework. It is extremely flexible as the name implies and it's simple to start using. But when the need is there, it can expand into a very sophisticated set of tools. It can be used individually or with teams. If you are already using one of the *Agile* platforms in a work context, this will build on something you already understand. If you're not familiar with *Agile*, this provides a brief introduction that may benefit you later.

For a primer on *Agile Scrum*, I recommend Jeff Sutherland's book, *Scrum – The Art of Doing Twice the Work in Half the Time*. This is not your typical time management book. For a deeper dive, download the *SBOK Guide* or *Scrum Body of Knowledge*. It's free online. For an introduction to *Lean*, I recommend, *A Factory of One* by Daniel Markovitz.

On the following pages, I'm going to offer a very basic overview of *Agile*. I'm going to share 6 components. They are **Kanban Board, Sprint, Sprint Planning, Daily Scrum, Sprint Review and Sprint Retrospective**. If you want to start simply, for personal job search, just focus on the *Kanban* Board. This will offer a super simple fast start. (I am intentionally capitalizing all the *Agile* specific language that may be new to you.)

Kanban Board

"Write the vision and make it plain on tablets, that he may run who reads it."
~Habakkuk 2:2

Great searchers use scoreboards and dashboards to stay aware of progress. Carl Pearson was the father of modern business statistics and is known for *Pearson's Law* which reads: "When performance is measured, performance improves". There is a corollary law that goes with it: "When performance is measured and reported, it improves exponentially". This is true even at the international economic level. The countries that measure and quantify have the strongest thriving economies.

In *Agile*, the project to-do list (called a Back-Log List) goes on a "Do" - "Doing" - "Done" board that is often referred to by the Japanese name *Kanban* (meaning "Card You Can See"). In the *Scrum* version, it goes by *ScrumBoard*.

I like the "Do" – "Doing" – "Done" format because it can provide a terrific job search check-in.

You can easily build your own *Kanban* on a sheet of paper, poster board or grease board with sticky notes. Several digital tools also work very well. Your Kanban columns can be set up on Microsoft *Excel, Apple Numbers* or *Google Sheets*. If spread sheets aren't your thing, a table can be set up in *Word, Pages or Docs*. If you go with the online option, *Trello.com* is terrific. It's easy to learn and can be reconfigured and shared easily. My current favorite is *Evernote which can be formatted within a single note, multiple notes or folders. Evernote is incredibly searchable and easily pulls up on all your devices. It also has a* sister program called *Kanbanote*.

I recommend using the low-tech or high-tech tool that you are already comfortable with. This will allow you to get organized quickly and stay focused on your job search.

Kanban Board

DO	DOING	DONE

Sprint

A Sprint is a time-boxed process of one month or less, where an individual or team implements a goal-oriented Backlog of Tasks. A common Sprint length is 21 days but it can be up to 30 days or as little as one week. If you're just introducing the concept, you can shorten your Sprint length to a single day or even an hour or less for a walk-through or training purposes.

The idea of a Sprint is to completely finish an increment of a project. A personal Sprint could be completing a chapter of a book, losing 5 pounds or exercising 30 minutes a day for 21 days. In job search, I have commonly worked with single day sprints focusing about 6 hours each on Strengths, Targets, Resumes, Interview Prep, and then about 6 hours on the 4 different search strategies. The second week is a sprint that is fully devoted to the Direct Contact strategy in the morning and the Employer Posting Application strategy in the afternoon.

The Sprint is all about having specific demonstrated results at the end. Some *Lean* practitioners use the term MVP for Minimum Viable Product to describe the end result. Minimum in this case does not refer to cutting corners or short cuts. It refers to delivering each project increment with a fully functional product or service. By keeping the Sprint length short, course corrections and customer responsive adjustments can be made. In job search, the organizations you are applying into are your customers.

Sprint Planning

Each Sprint begins with a planning session. In the world of software design, a planning session for a 21 day Sprint might take 8 hours. You may spend much less time if you're using the *Agile* method for personal job search. I recommend the 1-week Sprint time frame for individual use in the beginning. When planning a Sprint segment, consider the

S.P.R.I.N.T.S. acrostic below that is loosely built on the *Agile* pattern. Most of these ideas are pulled from the *Agile Scrum* family but some are pulled from *Lean*.

<u>S</u>tory Map

Agile planning begins with a focus on how the product/service will add value to a client, customer or specific end user. *Agile* planning starts with a 3-step User Story that is often placed on a simple 3x5 index card.

I am... Who is the client, customer or end user or what is their role? (Example: Secretary, Bookkeeper) In job search you will be focusing on the hiring manager who can employ you.

I want... What does the end user want the product/service to achieve for them? (Example: Word Processing, Spread Sheet) What is the hiring manager looking for? What talents, skills, specialized knowledge sets, values and character qualities are mission critical for them?

So that... What will be the benefit of that? (Example: Faster Document Preparation, Clear Accounting) What do those strengths in a potential employee help them accomplish?

In job search, the story map is best created from **informational interviews**. Sometimes we encourage a job search candidate to start their search process with informational interviews. There is no better way to find out what an employer is looking for.

A Story Map includes a description of what will be delivered to the client or customer. *Agile* planning is very big on providing a very clear definition of "Done". The "Done" criteria should include quality standards. (Example: Software will include intuitive keyboard short cuts and be field tested and approved by secretaries.)

Deliverables are what will be delivered and demonstrated at the end of each Sprint. *Agile* often creates a Project Vision Statement that explains the business need that will be met or what problem will be solved. (Example: We are creating a new software to enhance document preparation.)

The Shippable Product/Service or Deliverables are what will be demonstrated at the end of each Sprint. Story Maps are often used to give a visual outline of the product/service development sequence. This is similar to Storyboarding used by *Disney*. Value Stream Mapping may be used to identify non-value adding elements of a process. **In job search, you are the product.**

Problems

A S.W.O.T. (**S**trengths-**W**eaknesses-**O**pportunities-**T**rouble) Analysis or a Force Field Analysis may be incorporated to identify potential obstacles and trouble. Threats are risks that could affect a project in a negative manner. Either of these tools can be used to assess your job search. What part of the job search is your biggest strength? What is your biggest weakness? These tools can be used as an amplifier to understand what hiring managers are dealing with and how you might help.

Roles and Responsibilities

Agile planning then moves to identify the team members. A Skills Requirement Matrix or framework can be used to identify skill gaps and training requirements for the roles you are interested in.

Companies like *Toyota*, *Apple*, *Google* and *Facebook* look for Passion, Talent, Personality, Character and Values as well as Skill and Knowledge. I recommend constructing a Strengths Matrix to identify what/who is needed on the team. *Facebook* is widely known to use a key strengths based question as a signature part of their interview process:

"On your very best day at work – the day you come home and think you have the very best job in the world – what did you do that day?"

The answer to that question will help you discover if the job you're applying for fits and if it's a role where you can add value.

Increments – Implementation - Iterations

Agile planning uses the term Iteration to describe the incremental segments within each Sprint. A Backlog or to-do list is built to describe the sequential tasks and activities that will go into the Sprint. I recommend setting up a job search to-do list based on the sections and items in this book. Then go to work.

Niche Work Space

I include an emphasis on the space where the work will be done. *Agile Scrum* often refers to the work space as the **War Room**. It is optimally designed in a way that all team members can move freely, communicate and get their work done.

The *Lean* family uses the Japanese term **Gemba** when talking about the space where value is created. Gemba could be the factory floor, a construction site, a farm, the desk where you write, the classroom where you teach, or the territory where you sell. *You need a Job Search Gemba*. You need a space to work.

Time Estimate

Agile generally uses a unique approach to estimating time and effort requirements on each Sprint. For job search, I recommend assigning a time box for each segment including Strengths Clarification, Targeting, Resume Crafting, Interview Prep and the segments of job search itself. It's easy for some personalities to get stuck in preparation tasks like writing the perfect resume. It's easy for other personality types to rush out with no preparation at all.

Sprint Velocity is a term used to identify the rate at which the team can complete the work of a Sprint. Think about the time and speed you will commit to your search. Consider your Productive Sustainable Pace that can be maintained. I often work with clients on what I call *Full-Throttle Campaigns*. Often this means a few very focused days followed by easier ones.

S Framework

Agile Lean uses a methodology called *5S*. They have corresponding Japanese terms but the English terms are Sort, Set Up, Sweep, Standardize and Sustain.

Sort means throwing out useless or obsolete items and organizing the remaining items by frequency of use.

Set Up is arranging the tools and materials to promote a smooth workflow. In construction, I referred to this as staging the job.

Sweep is the maintenance phase and includes keeping the workspace clean. I would refer to it as *Struggle* because it's my weakness.

Standardize means developing a systematic ongoing work process. Standardizing in the *5S* sense is not static but open-ended, including ongoing improvements.

Sustain means having an ongoing system for maintaining and upgrading the first four elements.

Each of these 5 processes can be applied to job search, especially to the maintenance of your Gemba or work environment.

Daily *Scrum* (Stand Up Meeting)

Agile teams have daily 15 minute, standup meetings, often in front of the *Kanban* Board. *Trello* versions can be used for teams working remotely from different locations. The team reviews what was completed yesterday and previews what will be completed today. In some contexts, a set of 4 questions are used:

1. What has my team done since the last meeting?
2. What will my team do until the next meeting?
3. What are other teams counting on that remains undone?

4. What is the team doing that might affect other teams?

Some Scrum teams use a shorter 3 question model:

1. What did I complete yesterday?

2. What will I complete today?

3. What obstacles am I currently facing?

The Daily *Scrum* is a great idea if you're working with a job search coach. It provides a framework for accountability and progress.

Sprint Review

The Sprint Review meeting, is typically structured to last 1-4 hours and is scalable up or down depending on the length of the Sprint. The purpose is to demonstrate or present the deliverables, usually to the Product Owner. In a job search context, this would be a meeting with your coach, describing your sprint progress and accomplishments.

Sprint Retrospective

The Sprint Retrospective is typically structured to last one hour and is also scalable up or down depending on the length of the Sprint. The purpose is to review the process of that particular Sprint, identify what was learned, and suggest improvements for future Sprints.

Some *Agile* Sprints include a Retrospective Kanban with four categories: "Went Well", "Needs to Change", "Question & Discussion", "Action Items". These would be focused on the job search strategies being implemented.

Job Search Results

It is so easy to get lulled into believing that individuals can be replaced like parts in a machine. With people, there are wide variations in strengths and performance. This is true with job search.

Jeff Sutherland, co-founder of the *Scrum Project Management System* offers the following true story in his book titled *Scrum – The Art of Doing Twice the Work in Half the Time:*

Professor Stanley Eisenstat has been the instructor in the notoriously difficult, *Computer Science 323* course at *Yale University*.

Former student turned tech entrepreneur, Joel Spolsky wanted to know if there was any correlation between time spent on class projects and the grade received. Spolsky discovered there was no correlation, but the results were more interesting than that.

He found the fastest "A" students outpaced the slower "A" students by an incredible 10:1 margin. In other words, they were 10x faster on class projects and got just as good of a grade.

Like Professor Eisenstat's *Computer Science 323* class, there are wide variations in how long different people take to find work. Some people are very gifted for the job search process itself. Others are not. This should be factored into the job search planning from the beginning.

DREAM JOB!!!

"I'm lazy! I hate work! Hate hard work in all its forms! Clever shortcuts, that's all I'm about!"

~Eliezer Yudkowsky

Chapter 14
The *Stanford* Short Cut

When I was a kid, we were always looking for a short cut. Sometimes this turned out well and sometimes it didn't. Occasionally this meant going through a stranger's backyard. Sometimes there was a dog...

Earlier I mentioned the research of the *Boyer Management Group*. They believe there are approximately 2100 important pieces to a complete job search strategy. My book has intentionally been a very condensed book on job search. It summarizes thousands of pages I've read, thousands of hours listening to recordings and quite a few classes, training programs and certificates. Still, it's a lot of information to assimilate and apply. Some readers will need more information. I'm planning a whole series of books that dive deeper into many of these chapters. My coaching sessions and training programs already offer many more details.

Maybe you're not a reader and you want to move fast. Then this chapter is for you. It's 5 simple steps...

1. **Write out a strengths summary**. Include the type of jobs you have an intense interest in. Include your natural talents, learned skills and knowledge sets.

2. **Identify a job target type**. Write down carpenter, manager, sales person or whatever type of job your strengths point toward.

3. **Find the names of people doing that job right now**. Find the names of people who hire individuals doing that job right now. Make a list of these names along with contact information.

4. **Make contact.** Use the phone. Walk in. Email. Use the *LinkedIn* mail. Go talk to them. Ask questions. Ask about the "Story" of the person you're interviewing. Specifically ask about the strengths (talents and skills) of the people who are currently excelling at that type of work. Ask about their "SUCCESSPATH". How did they develop and grow in the work?

5. **Repeat and refine these steps until you get a job.**

That's it. Go for it....

The *Stanford* Short Cut

Stanford University offers a very popular life design class taught by Bill Burnett and Dave Evans. They are co-founders of the *Life Design Lab* at this prestigious university.

In their book, *Designing Your Life*, they share the job finding method offered in the course. They refer to it as *Job Prototyping* using *Life Design Interviews*.

The method outlines the strategy, beginning with asking people who work in your field of interest to share their life story or work story. It involves asking for a brief meeting to learn about the role this person performs to see if, at a later date, you might be interested in that work yourself. Bill and Dave maintain you should never go after a job, but go after the story.

After you spend the majority of the interview getting the story... ask a simple follow up question:

"What steps would be involved in exploring how someone like me might become part of this organization?"

That's it!

Don't ask for the job!

Ask about the steps involved!

Bill and Dave share the story of Kurt, who had master's degrees from both *Stanford* and *Yale*. Kurt had been banging his head against the wall with traditional job search strategies, applying online like everyone else, and getting no job offers.

Kurt agreed to try this Stanford short-cut and got 7 job offers in very short order. He didn't ask for the job in any of the interviews. He just asked for "the story" and then used "the steps" question. Kurt got his dream job! He works full-time, has flex-hours, a short commute, good money and work that is meaningful.

"I'll bet my autopsy reveals my mouth is too big."

~Bill Watterson

Chapter 15
The Autopsy

Some of the most successful television shows and novel characters have centered on the autopsy. When I was growing up Jack Klugman played *Quincy*. Patricia Cornwall's novels feature Dr. Kay Scarpetta and more recently we've had the *CSI* shows. Susy and I both like the quirky Max Bergman in the new iteration of *Hawaii Five-O*. The basic idea is to identify cause of death. In criminal cases, clues are discovered. In regular medicine the focus might be on learning, future prevention and an advancement in medicine that will save lives.

Much of my work has been deconstructing both successes and failures. When I was a sales manager I put together a "Lost Sale Autopsy" form that encouraged my team to reflect on their wins and losses looking for clues that might accelerate success. The tool walked them through the steps of our sales cycle presentation. As a group, salespeople aren't always the most reflective bunch and I seriously doubt it got a lot of use. But if you are serious about success in any arena, career, weight loss or even relationships; an autopsy can get you back on track.

Leadership expert John Maxwell shares, "Experience is <u>NOT</u> the best teacher. Evaluated experience is the best teacher." This is a core concept in the *Agile Project Management System* used at *Toyota* and other top organizations in many industries. In chapter 13 I wrote about both the *Sprint Review* and the *Sprint Retrospective*.

Most people don't really take the time to evaluate their experience and if they do, it's done in non-productive ways. Action oriented people may evaluate too little or not at all. Those of us who are thinkers may over evaluate and end up obsessing, brooding and depressed. There is a middle path!

One of the best things our *Road to Jobs* program provided was a place for candidates to evaluate their job search experiences and get what I call "feed-forward". Feedback is rarely useful.

Power of Positive Thinking author Norman Vincent Peale used to partner with a psychiatrist by the name of Smiley Blanton. Dr. Blanton said there was a huge difference between what he called "If Only" people and "Next Time" people. When evaluating their life, unhealthy unproductive people get stuck thinking, "If only I'd done this." "If only I'd done that." Healthy productive people often make as many mistakes, but they think, "Next time I'll do this." "Next time I'll do that." The most successful people do regularly glance in the rearview mirror, but most of the focus is forward. That's true with driving, it's true with life and it's true with job search.

This is a primary value of having a good career coach. A good coach will help you evaluate experience, give good feed-forward and keep you focused on next time.

During the *NFL* football season, I can promise you one thing. The day after each game will have a significant amount of time devoted to watching film from the previous performance. Every player will have been graded on every play with comments. The film will be viewed first by the coaches, then by offense or defense team and then by position.

The largest churches in America carefully review each of their weekend services to make sure they communicated what they wanted to communicate.

I started out this book saying I wanted to help you, "Rock Your Job Search". What if you spent just 10 minutes after every interview writing down your observations? Could you spend 5 minutes jotting down notes in an app like *Evernote* or on a 3x5 card after every direct contact meeting or networking event? Do you think you would get better?

Here's a checklist using steps in this book to do your own **post-interview autopsy** or analysis:

Was I clear on my **Stand-Out Strengths** and **Selling Points** including passion, talent, skills, knowledge, transferrable experience and how each could contribute on this job?

Was I clear on the job **Target?** Did I review and deconstruct the position description? Did I research the company's website and use other resources like *Glass Door?* Did I use *O*NET* as a resource to identify tasks, tools, abilities and skills etc…?

Did I have a customized **Resume Package** that included a targeted resume, cover letter, portfolio, references, endorsement and leave-behind sheets?

Did I prepare for this **Interview** with written talking points, appropriate clothing and a company research plan? Did I practice common questions like, "Tell Me About Yourself"?

Did I identify potential job search **Challenges** before the interview and think through solutions and management options?

What do I need to do **Next Time**?

You can also do a weekly autopsy or analysis based on your job search efforts. Again, you'll get the most benefit out of this if you have a good coach asking the questions and keeping you focused on the future.

Did I check my **Professional Email** messages daily?

Did I check my **Professional Voice Mail** daily? Is my box empty and ready for new messages?

Does my **Professional Wardrobe** need adjustment? Laundry? Cleaners?

Did I use the **Direct Contact** strategy approaching employers for hidden or un-posted jobs this week? How many?

Did I check *Craigslist* and *Indeed* for **Employer Postings?** Did I apply online in the most effective way possible?

Did I work on **Relationship Networking?** Did I attend any industry group meetings or meet ups? Did I maximize social media platforms like *LinkedIn*?

Did I register with **Search and Staffing** companies?

Did I identify, manage, solve or harness any job search **Challenges**?

Was I flexible? Did I improvise and swing into **Job Search Jazz**?

Did I organize and track my activity with *Agile* **Job Search Project** system using a *Kanban* Board? Did I plan any Sprints?

How is my **Job Search Office** working? Do I need to adjust my war room?

What's the **"Elephant in the Elevator"**? Am I ignoring something obvious… but important?

What are my **Job Search Strengths**? How can I better leverage them next week?

What are my **Job Search Weaknesses**? Can I outsource anything or get help? Do I need to practice something or develop more skills?

This last set of questions has actually been quite a source of discussion and even conflict in the *Road to Jobs* team meetings. This has largely been a family business. My dad (Allen Cobb) has consistently taken the position that the best way to do job search is through some form of **Direct Contact** as described in chapter 5. If a candidate is unwilling to do this, they can't continue in the program. While I agree that Direct Contact is the fastest and most effective way to get many or even most jobs, I believe that it is also the most frightening and difficult for most people. I also believe it's less effective with large companies who use a huge online screening apparatus.

I don't believe we will ever resolve this internal debate. What I do believe is that you need to identify your strengths and weaknesses as they relate to job search and play to your strengths as often as you can. You can accelerate this by doing some kind of regular autopsy or analysis.

"There are always door openings. And gradually, it accumulates. The opportunities open up in front of you."

~Buzz Aldrin

Afterword

Accumulation

Success strategist Brian Tracy talks about what he calls, "The Law of Accumulation". Tracy says, "Everything great and worthwhile in human life is an accumulation of hundreds and sometimes thousands of tiny efforts and sacrifices that nobody ever sees or appreciates...A snowball starts very small, but it grows as it adds millions and millions of tiny snowflakes, and continues to grow as it gathers momentum."

Your body of knowledge results from accumulating millions of small information pieces. Any person with a large knowledge base has spent thousands of hours building that knowledge one piece at a time. What you see when you meet that individual, is an expert in his or her field. It's that high level of knowledge that makes him extremely valuable in the marketplace.

Warren Buffett's daily routine includes a lot of reading. In fact, he spends about 80% of his day reading. And he does this *every* day. Buffett reportedly reads at least 3 annual reports (a couple of hundred pages each) every day. When asked how to get smarter he held up a stack of paper and said, "Read 500 pages like this every day. That's how knowledge builds up, like compound interest."

Accumulation applies in the area of experience. Successful people in any field are those who have far more experience in that field than the average. There is nothing that replaces experience. Nothing.

Good and bad job search activity accumulates. It compounds. You can waste time today and it may not make a big difference. You can probably waste time all week without a huge setback. It's like gaining weight. You can overeat today and the most you would gain would be a pound or so. Your clothes will still fit. Even your spouse wouldn't know the difference. But after 3 months of overeating, you will have put on some serious weight.

What you are doing right now turns into minutes. Minutes turn into hours into days into months into years into a lifetime into a legacy... even an eternity. Investment of job search time pays off over time.

Tolstoy spent 6 years writing *War and Peace*. Da Vinci worked on the *Mona Lisa* four years as did Michelangelo painting the ceiling of the *Sistine Chapel*. Most people overestimate what they can accomplish in a single year and underestimate what they can accomplish in five years. It's accumulation.

Poorly used time accumulates as well. According to *Digital Trends*, Americans are spending an average of 4.7 hours a day on social media, much of it on their phones. Some of this is happening during your job search and is task avoidance. This time accumulates.

Many people start a job search program and they don't stick with it.

Static and Dynamic Equilibrium

One problem with job search is that it doesn't stay managed. In past workshops, I would bring in a bowl and a marble. Set the marble in a right side up bowl and it will stay there. Set a marble in an upside down bowl and it will keep rolling off. The right side up bowl represents "Static Equilibrium". You set something up and it stays set up. The upside down bowl represents "Dynamic Equilibrium". For the marble to stay on top of the bowl, you must keep putting it back up there.

Job Search is a dynamic equilibrium activity. It doesn't stay managed. It's like weight management. You don't expect your good eating habits from last month to help with your weight management this month. You have to get up and take action every day.

Whenever I coach a client, present a training program or sit down to write a book chapter, I am acutely aware that life is so much more complicated than the best advice I could offer. Any single piece of wisdom is always incomplete. Most groupings of wisdom are incomplete as well. This book is actually shorter than the one I originally wrote. I became convinced that many in my intended audience wouldn't read a longer book, at least initially. So you have the shortened version with some of the material left on the "cutting room floor".

I am also aware that most readers who start a book, don't finish it and fewer still actually implement even one of the ideas presented. Obviously that won't help.

The *STRENGTHSPATH Job Search* is an integrated, interdependent set of strategies. My observation and experience is that they work together synergistically. Because you can't do everything at once, this book is laid out in a strategic sequence. Work through the first chapters to get a basic understanding of the different *Strength* components. Then begin working through the *Target* chapter. Move into the chapter on *Resume Writing* and *Interview Preparation*. You will run into roadblocks trying to merge the ideas. You will hit potholes and come to detours. But if you stay with it, I believe you'll find the on-ramp to your next job, and eventually, if you stay focused, your dream job.

I will close the book with one last thought. At the end of the day, job search is about making choices. Should I do this or that? Should I increase the time spent on one activity and decrease the time spent on another? In my own life, I find that God is willing to offer help with these decisions, including the little ones. As an imperfect follower of Jesus, I try to live my days in constant communication with God through the One referred to in Scripture as Holy Spirit. I frequently ask Him, "Should I do this or that?" Although I don't claim to hear an audible voice, somewhere deep in my spirit, I believe I get direction on matters both large and small.

I also try to spend part of every day reading and thinking about a section of Scripture. Susy and I usually start our day together in this way. I believe it grounds us, gets us on the same page with each other, and with God. The Bible is full of great career management tips. That's where I got my introduction to strengths. And it not only emphasizes the importance of priorities, but offers clear direction on what the priorities should be for a well-lived life.

When I was very young, my mother helped me memorize a short passage of Scripture from the book of Proverbs. Susy and I have that passage framed in our entry way. It reads, "Trust in the Lord with all your heart and don't lean on your own understanding. In all your ways acknowledge God and He will direct your paths."

~See You On The Path!!!

Dale Cobb

Bibliography

Prologue

1. Zig Ziglar, *See You At The Top* (Gretna, Louisiana: Pelican Publishing, 1977), 6.

2. Jim Clifton, *The Coming Job War* (New York: Gallup Press, 2011), 106.

3. Kip Tindell, *Uncontainable: How Passion, Commitment, and Conscious Capitalism Built a Business Where Everyone Thrives* (New York: Hachette Book Group, 2014), 53.

4. Debra L. Angel & Elisabeth H. Sanders-Park, *The 6 Reasons You'll Get the Job* (New York: Prentice Hall Press, 2010).

Success 101 – Getting Set Up

1. Nathan Gebhard, Brian McAllister and Mike Marriner with Jay Sacher, Alyssa Frank, Annie Mais, Jaime Zehler and Willie Witte, *Roadmap* (San Francisco: Chronicle Books, San Francisco, 2015).

Chapter 1   Your Signature Strengths

1. Oprah Winfrey, *The Best of Oprah's What I Know For Sure* (New York: The Oprah Magazine, Hearst Corporation, 2000), 39.

2. Howard Gardner, *Multiple Intelligences* (New York: Basic Books, New York, 1993), 17-26.

3. Margaret E. Broadley, *Your Natural Gifts* (McLean, Virginia: EPM Publications, 1977), 3-7.

4. Peter Drucker, *Managing Oneself* (Boston: Harvard Business Review, 2008),11-19.

5. Marcus Buckingham, *StandOut 2.0* (Boston: One Thing Productions/Harvard Business School Publishing, 2015), 8.

6. Stephen R. Covey with Rebecca Merrill, *The Speed of Trust* (New York: Free Press/Simon and Schuster, 2001).

7. Tom Rath and Barry Conchie, *Strengths Based Leadership* (New York: Gallup Press, 2008), 24.

8. Jim Loehr, *The Only Way To Win: How Building Character Drives Higher Achievement and Greater Fulfillment in Business and Life* (New York: Hyperion, 2012).

9. Dr. Caroline Leaf, *The Gift In You* (Nashville: Thomas Nelson, 2009).

10. Denis Waitley, *Being The Best* (Nashville: Oliver Nelson, 1987).

Chapter 2   Your Signature Targets

1. Kate Wendleton, *Targeting A Great Career* (Boston: Cengage Learning, 2014).

2. David P. Campbell, *If You Don't Know Where You're Going, You'll Probably End Up Somewhere Else* (Notre Dame: Soren Books, 2007).

3. Tony Robbins, *Unlimited Power: The Way to Peak Personal Achievement* (New York: Fawcett Columbine, 1986), 199.

4. Sean Aiken, *The One Week Job Project: 1 Man, 1 Year, 52 Jobs* (New York: Villard Books/Random House, 2010).

5. Laurence Shatkin and Michael Farr, *Overnight Career Choice: Discover Your Ideal Job in Just A Few Hours* 2nd Edition (Indianapolis: Jist Works, 2011).

6. Earl Nightingale, *The River or the Goal* (Chicago: Nightingale-Conant), http://www.nightingale.com/articles/the-river-or-the-goal/.

7. Interview with Diane Sawyer (*US Magazine*, 1997).

8. Richard N. Bolles, *What Color Is Your Parachute Job Hunter's Workbook* (Berkeley: 10 Speed Press, 2010).

9. Julie Jansen, *I Don't Know What I Want, But I Know It's Not This* (New York: Penguin, 2003).

10. Richard Eyre, *Spiritual Serendipity, Cultivating and Celebrating the Art of the Unexpected* (New York: Simon and Schuster, 1997).

11. Bobb Biehl, *Stop Setting Goals – If You Would Rather Solve Problems* (Nashville: Moorings Publishing, 1995).

12. Stephen R. Covey, *Seven Habits of Highly Effective People* (New York: Free Press, A Division of Simon & Schuster, 2004).

13. Victor Frankl, *Man's Search for Meaning* (Boston: Beacon Press, 2014).

14. Parker J. Palmer, *Let Your Life Speak: Listening for the Voice of Vocation* (San Francisco: Jossey-Bass, John Wiley & Sons, 2000), 3.

15. Brian Tracy, *Goals! How To Get Everything You Want – Faster Than You Ever Thought Possible* (San Francisco: Barrett Koehler, 2010).

16. Mark Lee, *How To Set Goals And Really Reach Them* (Portland: Horizon House, 1978).

17. Richard Nelson Bolles, *How To Find Your Mission In Life* (Berkeley: 10 Speed Press, 2000).

18. Timothy Butler, *Working with Symbolic Intelligence: The 100 Jobs Exercise* (Harvard Business School Exercise 812-064, December 2011).

Chapter 3   Your Signature Resume Package

1. Susan Whitcomb, *Resume Magic: Trade Secrets of a Professional Resume Writer* (Indianapolis: JIST Works, 2007).

2. Louise M. Kursmark and Wendy Enelow, *Modernize Your Resume* (Coleman Falls: Emerald Career Publishing, 2016).

3. Richard N. Bolles, *What Color Is Your Parachute? Guide To Rethinking Resumes* (Berkeley: 10 Speed Press, 2014).

4. Kate Wendleton, *Packaging Yourself: The Targeted Resume* (Boston: Cengage Learning, 2014).

5. Lea McLeod and Cheryl McLeod, *The Resume Coloring Book* (Portland: McLeod Studios, 2013).

6. Martin Yate, *Knock'em Dead Resumes 11th Edition* (Avon: Adams Media, 2014).

7. Dan Quillen, *The Perfect Resume* (New York: Simon & Schuster/Cold Springs Press, 2014).

8. Joyce Lain Kennedy, *Resumes for Dummies* (Hoboken: John Wiley & Sons, 2007).

9. Pat Criscito, *Resumes That Pop – Designs that Reflect Your Personal Brand (*Colorado Springs: Protoype Ltd, Barron's, 2010).

10. *The Ladders Guide To Crafting The Professional Resume* (New York: The Ladders), http://cdn.theladders.net/static/pdfs/Crafting_The_Professionals_Resume.pdf.

Chapter 4   Your Signature Interview

1. Kate Wendleton, *Mastering the Job Interview And Winning The Money Game* (Boston: Cengage Learning, 2014).

2. Susan Whitcomb, *Interview Magic: Job Interview Secrets from America's Career and Life Coach* (Indianapolis: JIST Works, 2008).

3. Richard N. Bolles, *What Color Is Your Parachute? Guide To Rethinking Interviews* (Berkeley: 10 Speed Press, 2014).

4. Daniel Porot with Frances Bolles Haynes, *The 101 Toughest Interview Questions...and Answers That Win the Job!* (Berkeley: 10 Speed Press, 2014).

5. Tony Beshara, *Acing The Interview: How to Ask and Answer the Questions That Will Get You the Job!* (New York: Amacom, 2008).

6. Paul C. Green, *Get Hired! – Winning Strategies To Ace The Interview* (Austin: Bard Press, 1996).

7. Alan Ladd, *DVD - Interview the Best* (Los Angeles: The Alan Ladd Group, 2008).

8. Joyce Lain Kennedy, *Job Interviews for Dummies* (Hoboken: John Wiley & Sons, 2012).

9. William Poundstone, *Are You Smart Enough to Work at Google?* (New York: Back Bay Books/Little Brown and Company, 2012).

Chapter 5   Direct Contact and Hidden Jobs

1. Donald Asher, *Cracking The Hidden Job Market-How To Find Opportunity In Any Economy* (Berkeley:10 Speed Press, 2011).

2. Susan Whitcomb, *Job Search Magic, Chapter 11 – Tap the Hidden Job Market with a Targeted Search* (Indianapolis: JIST Works, 2008), 273-318.

3. Laura M. Labovich, *101 Conversations for Career Success: Learn to Network, Cold Call and Tweet Your Way to Your Dream Job* (New York: Learning Express, 2012).

4. Brian Graham, *Get Hired Fast: Tap the Hidden Job Market in 15 Days* (Avon: Adams Media, 2005).

5. Harvey Mackay, *Use Your Head To Get Your Foot In The Door – Job Search Secrets No One Else Will Tell You* (New York: Portfolio/Penguin, 2010).

6. Irv Zuckerman, *Hire Power – The 6-Step Process to Get the Job You Need in 60 Days – Guaranteed* (New York: Perigee/Putnam, 1993).

Chapter 6   Employer Postings

1. Mark Emery Bolles and Richard Nelson Bolles, *Job-Hunting Online 6th Edition* (Berkeley: 10 Speed Press, 2011).

Chapter 7   Relationship Networking

1. Joshua Waldman, *Job Searching with Social Media for Dummies* (Hoboken: John Wiley & Sons, 2011).

2. Joshua Waldman with Dr. Sean Harry, *The Social Media Job Search Workbook* (Tigard: Career Enlightenment, 2014).

3. Wayne Breitbarth, *The Power Formula for LinkedIn Success* (Austin: Greenleaf Book Group, 2013).

4. Dan Schawbel, *Me 2.0: 4 Steps to Building Your Future* (New York: Kaplan, 2010).

5. David McNally and Karl D. Speak, *Be Your Own Brand* (San Francisco: Barrett Koehler, 2011).

6. Seth Godin, *Tribes: We Need You To Lead Us* (New York: Portfolio/Penguin, 2008).

7. David Arvin, *It's Not Who You Know, It's Who Knows You* (Castle Rock: Classified Press, 2014).

8. Joel Comm, *Twitter Power* (Hoboken: John Wiley & Sons, 2009).

Chapter 8   Staffing and Search Firms

1. Cathy A. Reilly, *The Temp Factor for Job Seekers: The Job Seeker's Guide to Temporary Employment* (Boca Raton: Universal Publishers, 2012).

Chapter 9   Search Challenges

1. Elisabeth H. Sanders-Park, *WorkNet Solutions: Career Development Tools & Training for the Real World* (Wilmington: WorkNet Solutions, 2009).

2. Debra L. Angel & Elisabeth H. Sanders-Park, *No One is Unemployable* (Covina: WorkNet Solutions, 1997).

3. Jane Marla Robbins, *Acting Techniques For Everyday Life* (New York: Marlowe and Company, 2002).

4. Susan Cain, *Quiet: The Power of Introverts in a World That Can't Stop Talking* (New York: Broadway Paperbacks/Random House, 2013).

5. Paul G. Stoltz and Erik Weihenmayer, *The Adversity Advantage: Turning Everyday Struggles Into Everyday Greatness* (New York: Fireside Press/Simon & Schuster, 2010).

6. Ryan Holiday, *The Obstacle Is The Way: The Timeless Art Of Turning Trials Into Triumph* (New York: Portfolio/Penguin, 2014).

7. Robert Schuller, *Tough Times Never Last, But Tough People Do* (New York: Bantam Books, 1984).

8. Seth Godin, *The Dip: A Little Book That Teaches You When To Quit (And When To Stick)* (New York: Portfolio/Penguin, 2007).

9. Annabelle Gurwitch, *DVD – Fired!: Tales of the Canned, Canceled, Downsized and Dismissed* (Los Angeles: Shout! Factory Music Company, 2007).

10. Richard Nelson Bolles and Susan Dale Brown, *Job-Hunting for the So-Called Handicapped or People Who Have Disabilities* (Berkeley: 10 Speed Press, 2001).

11. Carol Christen and Richard Nelson Bolles with Jean M. Blomquist, *What Color Is Your Parachute? For Teens* (Berkeley: 10 Speed Press, 2010).

12. Gayle Backstrom, *I'd Rather Be Working: A Step-by-Step Guide to Financial Self-Support for People with Chronic Illness* (New York: Amacom, 2002).

13. Lisa Johnson Mandell, *Career Comeback: Repackage Yourself to Get the Job You Want* (New York: Springboard Press, 2010).

Chapter 10 Job Shifting

1. Steve Harvey, *Act Like A Success Think Like A Success* (New York: Amistad/Harper Collins, 2014), 77-80.

Chapter 11 Job Shaping

1. Amy Wrzesniewski, Justin M. Berg and Jane E. Dutton, *Managing Yourself: Turn the Job You Have into the Job You Want* (Boston: Harvard Business Review, June 2010) https://hbr.org/2010/06/managing-yourself-turn-the-job-you-have-into-the-job-you-want .

2. Amy Wrzesniewski, Justin M. Berg and Jane E. Dutton, *The Job Crafting Booklet* (Ann Arbor: University of Michigan, June 2010).

3. Nick Tasler, *Help Your Best People Do A Better Job* (New York: Bloomberg, 2010), http://www.bloomberg.com/news/articles/2010-03-26/help-your-best-people-do-a-better-job .

4. Google's Re: Work Seminar, *Job Crafting - Amy Wrzesniewski On Creating Meaning In Your Own Work* (YouTube, Nov 10, 2014).

5. Marcus Buckingham, *The Truth About You – Your Secret To Success* (Nashville: Thomas Nelson, 2008).

6. Marcus Buckingham, *Go Put Your Strengths To Work – 6 Powerful Steps To Achieve Outstanding Performance* (New York: Free

Press/Simon & Schuster, 2007).

7. Joan Biskupic, *Personalities Shape Questioning* (USA Today, October 19, 2009),
http://www.usatoday.com/printedition/news/20091019/courtargues19_st.art.htm .

8. Michael Burleigh, *An American Triple Threat: Eisenhower, Patton, and Bradley* (Wall Street Journal, April, 2011),
http://online.wsj.com/article/SB1000142405274870380630457623663336219 9332.html .

9. Robert Schuller, *If It's Going To Be It's Up To Me* (San Francisco: Harper), 138.

10. Johnny Carson Quote,
http://www.quotationspage.com/quote/2965.html .

11. Patrick McGinnis, *The 10% Entrepreneur* (New York: Portfolio/Penguin/Random House, 2016).

12. Rick Smith, *The Leap* (New York: Portfolio/Penguin/Random House, 2009).

13. Jack Welch with Suzy Welch, *Winning* (New York: Harper Collins, 2005).

Chapter 12   Job Search Jazz

1. Eric Abrahamson and David H. Freedman, *A Perfect Mess* (New York: Back Bay/Little Brown & Company, 2007).

2. Herbie Hancock, *Possibilities DVD* (New York: Vector Recordings, April 18, 2006).

3. Wynton Marsalis with Geoffrey C. Ward, *Moving to Higher Ground – How Jazz Can Change Your Life* (New York: Random House, 2008).

4. Robert Gelinas, *Finding the Groove - Composing A Jazz-Shaped Faith* (Grand Rapids: Zondervan, 2009).

Chapter 13   Agile Project Management Job Search

1. Hirotaka Takeuchi and Ikujiro Nonaka, *The New New Product Development Game (*Boston: Harvard Business Review, January 1986),
https://hbr.org/1986/01/the-new-new-product-development-game .

2. Tycho Press, *Scrum Basics: A Very Quick Guide to Agile Project Management* (Berkeley: Tycho Press, 2015).

3. Jeff Sutherland, *Scrum: The Art of Doing Twice the Work in Half the Time* (New York: Crown Business, 2014).

4. Tridibesh Satpathy - Lead Author, *Scrum Study: A Guide to the Scrum*

Body of Knowledge (Phoenix: Scrumstudy, 2013).

5. *"Write the vision and make it plain on tablets, that he may run who reads it."* This passage from Habakkuk 2:2 is taken from the New King James Version published by Thomas Nelson.

6. Jim Benson, Tonianne DeMaria Barry, *Personal Kanban: Mapping Work | Navigating Life* (Seattle: Modus Operandi Press, 2009).

7. Daniel Markovitz, *A Factory of One: Applying Lean Principles to Banish Waste and Improve Personal Performance* (Boca Raton: CRC Press, 2012).

Chapter 14   The Stanford Short Cut

1. Bill Burnett and Dave Evans, *Designing Your Life: How To Build A Well-Lived, Joyful Life* (New York: Alfred Knopf, 2016), 146-149.

Chapter 15   The Autopsy

1. Norman Vincent Peale, *Why Some Positive Thinkers Get Powerful Results* (New York: Random House, 1987).

Afterword

1. Brian Tracy, *The Great Little Book On Universal Laws of Success* (Franklin Lakes, Career Press, 1997), 74.

Further Reading

To write this book, I've stood on a lot of other people's shoulders. I am approaching 2000 books in my human potential and career development library. A few hundred are relevant to job search. Listed below are around 100 of the best references I own and recommend for their wisdom in the steps and categories used in this book. A single book can never include everything you need to know. If you are building a career, it would be valuable to start your own library. If you are in job search mode, a few of these resources will add depth to what I've said on the subject. If you work anywhere in the career services or career development field you are cheating your clients by not acquainting yourself with the thinking, strategies and experiences of other experts in the field. The resources below are a good start!

Recommended General Job Search Books

Job Search Magic, Susan Whitcomb (Extremely comprehensive job search guide. Whitcomb is perhaps the most thorough researcher and writer in the job search field.)

What Color Is Your Parachute?, Richard Bolles (Best selling job search book of all time with a new addition coming out every year. Based on his work with over 40,000 individuals, this book has probably helped more people identify and obtain their dream job than any other single resource in history. It's a classic!)

Graduate Employment Preparedness Assessment Development Guide, Hank Boyer (This volume is encyclopedic and explains more than 2,100 job search best practices. A must for career service professionals!)

Knock'em Dead Job Search, Martin Yate (I recommend all of Yate's books. I love his *Competitive Difference Questionnaire* and his *Position*

Description Deconstruction approach. Like Richard Bolles, he updates his books frequently… My only problem is that sometimes useful strategies are removed.)

Zen And The Art Of Making A Living, Laurence Boldt (This book is a classic in the field. No career library is complete without it.)

The Job Search Solution, Tony Beshara (Beshara is Dr. Phil McGraw's go-to expert on job search and the 33 Myths in the book challenge common assumptions with typical Dr. Phil bluntness. Toward the end, the book has a great chapter on overcoming employer biases.)

The 2-Hour Job Search – Using Technology to Get The Right Job Faster, Steve Dalton (Dalton is the Senior Career Consultant at *Duke University's Fuqua School of Business*. This book is really unique and hard to categorize. The book's strength is job search organization but there's more than that.)

Use Your Head To Get Your Foot In The Door – Job Search Secrets No One Else Will Tell You, Harvey Mackay (I recommend all of Harvey's books!)

48 Days To The Work You Love, Dan Miller (This book and the program it's based on has been recommended by financial guru Dave Ramsey for years. It's terrific!)

6 Reasons You'll Get The Job, Debra Angel MacDougall and Elisabeth Harney Sanders-Park (Richard Bolles says in the forward that these two offer absolutely fresh perspectives in the job search field. They do and it's a MUST READ!)

Absolutely Abby's 101 Job Search Secrets, Abby Kohut (Abby did a workshop for the career college where I was working as a career services coordinator. Easy to read – solid advice.)

The Robert Half Way to Get Hired in Today's Job Market, Robert Half (This book was published in 1963 and many elements are out of date. Still, I have a bias toward anything from Robert Half and the companies he started. This book is worth looking for in used bookstores.)

Job Hunting For Dummies, Max Messmer (As of this writing, Max has been the CEO of the *Robert Half Companies* mentioned above for over 20 years. Max has some unique advice to offer - like the section on setting up a job search headquarters.)

Guerrilla Marketing For Job Hunters 2.0, Jay Conrad Levinson and David E. Perry (At the end of the day, Job Search is Sales! This is part of a book series by a guy who understands sales and marketing as well as anyone in the country. It is full of tips and takes on job search you won't find anywhere else.)

Recommended Strengths Based Career Selection Books

Your Natural Gifts, Margaret Broadley (This book, recommended by Denis Waitley, was my first introduction to selecting a career based on aptitudes. Everyone should read the book and go to *Johnson O'Conner* and take their two day work sample assessment.)

Learning To Use Your Aptitudes, Dean Trembly (Dean was on staff at Cal Poly in San Luis Obispo. This book was another assessable introduction to the Johnson O'Conner aptitudes.)

The Pathfinder, Nicholas Lore (Brilliant! Lore has commendations from two U.S. Presidents. This book served as a model for my own book, *The STRENGTHSPATH Principle*. He does a good job of identifying many kinds of strengths and applying them to career selection.)

Now, What?, Nicholas Lore & Anthony Spadafore (Another brilliant book…This one is similar to *The Pathfinder* but slanted toward a younger generation.)

Great Work – Great Career, Stephen R. Covey and Jennifer Colosimo (A personal favorite. Great introduction to strengths and careers. Extremely accessible and easy to read.)

How To Find The Work You Love, Laurence Boldt (My whole copy is highlighted.)

The Person Called You: Why You're Here, Why You Matter and What Should You Do With Your Life, Bill Hendricks (An incredibly helpful book that recommends the *Autobiography* and *Achievement List* methods of strengths discovery.)

Why You Can't Be Anything You Want to Be, Arthur Miller Jr. with William Hendricks (I love Arthur Miller's approach to strengths.)

Career Satisfaction and Success, Bernard Haldane (Haldane was arguably the top career planning guy in the 1950's and 1960's. His books are timeless and I love them all! This one introduces the *SIMS – System to Identify Motivated Skills*.)

How to Make a Habit of Success, Bernard Haldane (Haldane was an advocate of a strengths discovery tool that utilized *Achievement List Analysis* along with a 52 item grid he called *Dynamic Success Factors*.)

Young Adult Career Planning, Bernard Haldane

Job Power Now!, Bernard Haldane

Unlocking Your Sixth Suitcase, John Bradley and Jay Carty (Bradley's talent assessment was one of my early introductions to ideas around talent. I don't believe that it ever got the recognition it deserved.)

If You Don't Know Where You're Going, You'll Probably End Up Somewhere Else, David P. Campbell (A classic in the field and one of the first career selection books I ever read.)

The Element, Ken Robinson (I think *The Element* is one of the best strengths books in print. Robinson also writes from decades of experience working as a reformer in education. If you haven't watched Robinson's *Ted Talks* do it now!)

The Acorn Principle, Jim Cathcart (This book was something of a model for my book *The STRENGTHSPATH Principle*. Cathcart does a wonderful job of identifying different kinds of strengths. Many of these are important but go unaddressed by most strengths practitioners.)

7 Kinds of Smart, Thomas Armstrong (Armstrong is the best interpreter of Howard Gardner's work on *Multiple Intelligence* theory at *Harvard University*. If strengths are embraced in an educational setting, it's often because of Armstrong's work making Gardner's thinking more accessible for the rest of us.)

What's Your Genius?, Jay Niblick (This book is an under discovered gem. Niblick gets talent and he's an expert on personality and values. Tony Robbins uses Jay's assessments for his coaching programs.)

Unique Ability 2.0, Dan Sullivan, Catherine Nomura, Julia Waller & Shannon Waller (This book is part of a whole suite of resources designed primarily for the entrepreneur. I love this stuff!)

Soar With Your Strengths, Donald O. Clifton & Paula Nelson (This book was one of my first introductions to strengths when it came out in 1992. Don designed the first Strengthfinder assessment with Marcus Buckingham later on. Don led the *Gallup* organization into the strengths arena and they've published numerous books on the topic, all of which should be devoured.)

Managing Oneself, Peter F. Drucker (Drucker is known for his writing on management. Only those who have actually read his books understand how deeply he was committed to strengths based career principles. This short book began as an article and was then republished. In it are some of the best explanations of strengths concepts that are available.)

The Effective Executive, Peter F. Drucker (Read the chapters titled, *What Can I Contribute* and *Making Your Strengths Productive.* Drucker is one of the few writer/thinkers who make a solid connection between contribution and strengths.)

Recommended Career Targeting Books

The New Quick Job-Hunting Map – How To Create A Picture Of Your Ideal Job or Next Career, Richard Nelson Bolles (A quick workbook to help with job targeting.)

What Color Is Your Parachute? Job Hunter's Workbook, Richard Nelson Bolles (Starts off with Bolles' take on the Autobiography strategy. This is a solid workbook that will help you get some direction in a weekend.)

Overnight Career Choice, Lawrence Shatkin, Ph.D. & Michael Farr

(This workshop in a book has great exercises but I doubt you'll make it through them overnight.)

Born For This: How To Find The Work You Were Meant To Do, Chris Guillebeau (I like Guillebeau's Joy-Money-Flow model, his material on social scripts, and I love the self-taught yoga instructor story.)

Getting Unstuck: A Guide to Discovering Your Next Career Path, Timothy Butler (I am taken with Butler's brilliant 100 Jobs exercise. It's a great short cut for someone not willing to spend adequate time with self discovery and strengths. It's also a great first move following strengths discovery exercises, especially when the jobs are connected to *O*NET* resources.)

Targeting A Great Career, Kate Wendleton (Published by the *5 O'Clock Club*, this book is part of a terrific series. They emphasize a version of the Autobiography strategy called *Seven Stories.*)

How to Find Your Mission in Life, Richard Bolles (Very short and thought provoking. Bolles sometimes includes it at the end of *What Color Is Your Parachute?)*

Your Dream Career For Dummies, Carol L. McClelland, Ph.D. (I like how Carol has used Howard Gardner's *Multiple Intelligence* theory in this book and connected it to career selection. I'm not aware of another resource that has made this connection so well.)

If You Don't Know Where You're Going, You'll Probably End Up Somewhere Else, David P. Campbell (A classic in the field and one of the first career selection books I ever read.)

Choosing a Vocation, Frank Parsons, Ph.D. (Published in 1909, this may be the first American book designed to help with career choice. It's still relevant today. I love Parson's intake questionnaire. The volume serves to establish a sense of history for those working as career service professionals.)

Making Vocational Choices: A Theory of Careers, John L. Holland (*The Holland Assessment* is used by many career advisors. His six career environments – realistic, investigative, artistic, social, enterprising and conventional are not super granular but they offer some good basic direction.)

Business Model You: A One-Page Method for Reinventing Your Career, Tim Clark, Alexander Osterwalder and Yves Pigneur (This book and the program it's based on offers a great way of visualizing the components of your career.)

The One-Week Job Project, Sean Aiken (While the rest of us wander around in an unemployed stuper, Sean managed to land a new job every week for a year. There is a companion DVD that adds depth and credibility to the book. The film should be shown to every high school senior and everyone about to graduate from college.)

Recommended Resume Package Books

Resume Magic, Susan Whitcomb (The most complete treatment of resumes available.)

Modernize Your Resume – Get Noticed... Get Hired, Louise M. Kursmark & Wendy Enelow (Great information on the most current trends. Any resume book by Kursmark or her partner Wendy Enelow is worthwhile.)

Knock'em Dead Resumes, Martin Yate (I love his *Competitive Difference Questionnaire* and his *Position Description Deconstruction* approach.)

Knock'em Dead Cover Letters, Martin Yate (In some editions Yate displays a side-by-side table showing how a candidate can clearly connect position description requirements with their own qualifications. I've successfully used the idea myself and on occasion modified the idea to use as a post interview leave behind. Hiring managers love it and I love Martin Yate's creativity.)

The Resume Coloring Book, Lea McLeod and Cheryl McLeod (Don't let the title deceive you! This is a great book for someone who wants to write their own resume. I love the "Interview Leave Behind" piece these two recommend. That alone is worth the price of the book.)

Resumes That Pop!, Pat Criscito (My current favorite book of resume samples. Very visually creative but not very applicant tracking software friendly.)

Packaging Yourself – The Targeted Resume, Kate Wendleton (Part of the excellent *5 O'Clock Club* Series.)

The Perfect Resume, Dan Quillen (Written by a former HR Professional. This book has a great section on how to list accomplishments.)

The Ladders Guide To Crafting The Professional Resume, The Ladders Staff (This amazing resource is available free online as a pdf.) https://cdn.theladders.net/static/pdfs/Crafting_The_Professionals_Resume.pdf

What Color Is Your Parachute? Guide To Rethinking Resumes, Richard Bolles (He is the go-to job search expert of my lifetime. Still, I don't think a resume is the area where he is the most knowledgeable.)

Same Day Resume, Louise M. Kursmark (Great workbook, short and easy to use.)

Job!, Rick Gillis (Great section on putting together an "Accomplishments Worksheet".)

Recommended Interview Preparation Books

Interview Magic, Susan Whitcomb (Like her other books, this book is encyclopedic leaving no interview stone unturned.)

Get Hired! Winning Strategies To Ace The Interview, Paul C. Green (I particularly like Green's chapter and diagram on the Four Interview Styles.)

Acing The Interview – How to Ask and Answer the Questions That Will Get You the Job!, Tony Beshara (I like the way this book categorizes the questions in chapters that allude to underlying questions that are never asked directly… Can you do the job? Do I like you? Are you a risk?)

Are You Smart Enough To Work At Google? – Trick Questions, Zen-

like Riddles, Insanely Difficult Puzzles and Other Devious Interviewing Techniques You Need to Know to Get a Job Anywhere in the New Economy, William Poundstone (Gets the award for longest sub-title! Companies are increasingly trying to figure out ways to insure they are hiring better employees. This book is probably worth reading especially if you're trying to get a job with a prominent tech company.)

What Color Is Your Parachute? Guide To Rethinking Interviews, Richard Bolles (Short and solid! I love the graphic that describes the best time in the interview process to negotiate salary.)

The 101 Toughest Interview Questions… and Answers That Win the Job!, Daniel Porot with Frances Bolles Haynes (This book is part of the "Parachute" family franchise of books. It's a good resource.)

Recommended Direct Contact & Hidden Job Market Books

Cracking The Hidden Job Market, Donald Asher (This book offers some of the most practical tips on making direct contacts into the hidden job market. Asher's 4-Steps: Identify a target of interest, Find someone doing that job right now, Talk to him/her, Repeat until hired is simple, doable and gets the fastest results in any job market. It also takes a certain amount of courage.)

Get Hired Fast – Tap The Hidden Job Market in 15 Days, Brian Graham (Graham's 50 contacts, 8 connections and 1 interview is very realistic. I prefer face-to-face approaches but the author's phone scripts and scenario responses are doable.)

Hire Power – The 6-Step Process To Get The Job You Need in 60 Days – Guaranteed, Irv Zuckerman (This book is older but the information on creating an *Achievement Dossier* and *Initiating Contact Conversations* are terrific.)

Unlock The Hidden Job Market, Duncan Mathison & Martha I. Finney (Great information on the hidden job market. I especially recommend chapter 6: *Make Passion Your Most Competitive Asset.*)

100 Conversations for Career Success, Laura M. Labovich & Miriam

Salpeter (Very practical step-by-step formulas handling face-to-face job search related meetings. Cold call strategies, informational interviewing and networking meetings are covered. The authors also have bonus chapters on connecting with social media.)

Recommended Employer Application Books

Job Hunting Online, Mark Emery Bolles & Richard Nelson Bolles (It's hard to find a job search expert who believes that applying for jobs online is a good strategy. In my opinion, it should be part of a well-rounded strategy. This is probably the best book on the topic.)

Recommended Networking Books

Tribes, Seth Godin (Seth Godin is one of my favorite authors and this is one of my favorite books. If you want to excel in your career and/or job search you need to find your tribe… your people. This book explains the concept.)

Promote Yourself – The New Rules for Career Success, Dan Schawbel (Good information on building a network and great information on developing and describing hard skills, soft skills and knowledge/expertise.)

Me 2.0, Dan Schawbel (This book is about building your brand, meaning your reputation.)

The Power Formula for LinkedIn Success, Wayne Breitbarth (This has been my favorite book on *LinkedIn*. Just before this writing, *LinkedIn* made major changes and I'm betting that a 4th edition is in the works.)

It's Not Who you Know, It's Who Knows You!, David Avrin (I love Arvin's title and the book doesn't disappoint.)

Job Searching with Social Media For Dummies, Joshua Waldman (Joshua is the go-to expert for all things social media as it relates to job search.)

The Social Media Job Search Workbook, Joshua Waldman (This book is much shorter and more accessible than Waldman's book from the

Dummies series. Start here.)

The Harvey Mackay Rolodex Book, Harvey Mackay (Written in 1993 before the age of computer databases, this short book still offers some of the best wisdom on building and maintaining relationships.)

Recommended Staffing Service Books

The Temp Factor – The Job Seeker's Guide To Temporary Employment, Cathy A. Reilly (There aren't a lot of books with advice in this category. Most candidates overlook staffing services as a path to permanent employment. But many companies use staffing services and search firms almost exclusively to pre-screen candidates. Don't close yourself off to this option.)

Recommended Search Challenge Books

No One is Unemployable, Debra L. Angel & Elisabeth H. Sanders-Park (The best of the search challenge books. It covers 70 plus barriers to employment with solid advice on how to manage them.)

Job-Hunting for the So-Called Handicapped or People Who Have Disabilities, Richard Bolles & Dale Susan Brown (I recommend starting with the straight talk. Bolles and Brown share four myths about the *ADA – American Disabilities Act*. There is a lot of misinformation and false expectations around this legislation and they do a good job of clearing it up.)

Getting Unstuck, A Guide To Discovering Your Next Career Path, Timothy Butler (One of the few books I've listed in multiple categories. Butler is a *Harvard Career Services* guy who spends the first part of the book helping readers understand ways they get stuck and some strategies for moving forward.)

The Career Guide for Creative and Unconventional People, Carol Eikleberry (I'm unconventional myself and found this book offers useful ideas for those of us who march to a different drummer. I particularly like the guided imagery exercise.)

Career Comeback – Repackage Yourself to Get The Job You Want,
Lisa Johnson Mandell (Great advice for those who need to hit the re-
fresh button on everything and are unacquainted with modern job
search. I love her list – 12 items you need to throw away now and 20
ways to raise your "Hip Quotient".)

*I'd Rather Be Working – A Step-By-Step Guide to Financial Self-
Support for People with Chronic Illness*, Gayle Backstrom (We've had
two young people in our family with chronic Lyme Disease and one with
cancer. I've also worked professionally with people who are suffering
from a variety of disabilities but who still want to work. This book spends
too much time on the legal issues for my taste but it's still a great
resource.)

Quiet – The Power of Introverts in a World That Can't Stop Talking,
Susan Cain (As a thinker, an introvert and sometimes shy person, I
recommend any of Susan's writings and talks.)

Acting Techniques For Everyday Life, Jane Marla Robbins (Oprah
Winfrey began her career pretending to be Barbara Walters until she
could find her own voice. I've made many sales calls playacting in
character. This is a great strategy for those who suffer from the thought
of interviewing.)

We Got Fired! ... And It's the Best Thing That Ever Happened to Us,
Harvey MacKay (A great resource for those who just got fired and a
great gift to give someone who just got fired.)

*The Job Hunter's Survival Guide – How to Find Hope and
Rewarding Work, Even When "There Are No Jobs"*, Richard Nelson
Bolles (Written in 2009 specifically for those who found themselves
unemployed due to the *Great Recession*. This book offers hope and
strategies for those layed off in one of the down economies we have
every 7-10 years.)

Recommended Job Shaping Books

The Truth About You, Marcus Buckingham (The shortest of the Buckingham books written to young adults. The original packaging came with a *Love It – Loathe It* activity recording book and a 20 minute excerpt from Buckingham's excellent film series, *Trombone Player Wanted.)*

Go Put Your Strengths To Work, Marcus Buckingham (The full companion to the *Trombone Player Wanted* film series. It focuses on crafting an existing job much more heavily than career selection. It also moves away from assessments and focuses on activating strengths based tasks and activities.)

Stand Out 2.0, Marcus Buckingham (*Stand Out 2.0* is an explanation of the assessment bearing the same name. Both are a 9 theme, less granular simplification of the 34 theme *Strengthfinder* assessment that Buckingham co-wrote with Don Clifton.)

Now, Discover Your Strengths, Marcus Buckingham (The original explanation of the 34 Theme *Strengthsfinder* 1.0. Strengthsfinder is designed to help one dial in their best approach to an existing job. It is not designed to be a career selection tool.)

Strengthsfinder 2.0, Tom Rath (The follow up explanation of the new *Strengthfinder* version.)

The Job Crafting Exercise Book, Justin M. Berg, Jane E. Dutton and Amy Wrzesniewski (Great explanation of the job crafting concept with real world examples.)

Recommended Agile Planning Books

Scrum, Jeff Sutherland (This is my favorite introduction to *Agile* and the version called *Scrum*. Great stories from varied industries fleshing out the concepts and strategies.)

Personal Kanban, Jim Benson (Simple introduction to *Agile* and the version called *Kanban*. It applies the concepts and strategies for individual use and personal productivity in any environment.)

A Factory of One, Daniel Markovitz (Simple introduction to *Agile* and the version called *Lean*.)

Also by Dale Cobb

The STRENGTHSPATH Principle: Your Roadmap to Career Success

The STRENGTHSPATH Time Manager

Look for these coming titles in the SUCCESSPATH Series:

The STRENGTHSPATH Guide to Selection and Hiring

The SUCCESSPATH Strategies: A Guide To Universal Success Principles

The STRENGTHSPATH Strategies: Succeeding by Doing What You Do Best

Crazy Good: A STRENGTHSPATH Guide to Discovering Your Natural Talents

Insanely Great: A STRENGTHSPATH Guide to Developing Your Talents Into Strengths

Wildly Successful: A STRENGTHSPATH Guide to Delivering Your Strengths in the Workplace

The STRENGTHSPATH Manager & Leader

The STRENGTHSPATH Sales Person

The STRENGTHSPATH Parent

Maximize Your Ministry: A STRENGTHSPATH Guide to Doing What You Do Best

The STRENGTHSPATH Educator

The Daily STRENGTHSPATH

SUCCESSPATH Sprint Coaching

One-to-One Sprints ☆ 60-Minute Seminars ☆ Workshops

Modeling Projects ☆ Performance Research

Strengths Assessments ☆ Selection ☆ Outplacement

Strengths Oriented Career Development Sprints
Arrive! - Strengths Oriented Goal Sprints
Strengths Oriented Time Management Sprints
"A-Game" Sprints
Service Oriented Selling Sprints
Storyboarding – Customer Experience Journey Sprints

Connect Online

Follow Our SUCCESSPATH Sixty Second Seminars

LinkedIn https://www.linkedin.com/in/dalecobb

Facebook
https://www.facebook.com/successpathcareerdevelopment/

Twitter https://twitter.com/strengthspath

Website http://www.successpathcareerdevelopment.com

Vimeo https://vimeo.com/dalecobb

YouTube https://www.youtube.com/user/daleacobb

Tumblr https://www.tumblr.com/blog/dalecobb

Contact

Dale Cobb
P.O. Box 870
Grover Beach, CA 93483
805.668.9600

Strengths Definitions

Contribution (Result, Benefit, Added Value, Difference Maker, Helpfulness, Significance, Deliverables, Profit, Performance, Solutions) Contribution is what you provide that helps attain an end result. It's the positive change that happens when you walk in the room, when you join a business unit, team or organization.

Passion (Intense Interests, Enthusiasm, Desire, Ambition, Love, Fascinations, Magnificent Obsession, Energy, Excitement) Passions are activities and subjects that make you feel strong. They may include willingness to sacrifice and suffer.

Talent (Natural Ability, Aptitude, Gift, Knack, Flair, Bent, Instinct, Genius, Inclination, Brilliance, Forte, Aptness) Talent is innate ability making performance and excellence at specific tasks easier. It also makes skill and knowledge acquisition easier with a specific domain.

Personality (Temperament, Preferences, Style, Nature, Disposition, Traits, Persona, Psyche) Personality is the organization of an individual's distinct traits and temperament.

Values (Priorities, Motivation, Beliefs, Ideals, What's Important) Values combine to build culture within an organization.

Learning Style (Perception, Organization, Retention and Response to Instruction Methods) Your learning path is your optimized pattern of acquiring and processing information.

Knowledge (General Vocabulary, Professional Language, Industry Terminology, Rules, Regulations, Laws, Principles, Theories) Knowledge is acquired information, facts, understanding and comprehension of a subject.

Skills (Developed Ability, Mastery, Proficiency, Competency, Know-How, How-To's including Methods, Steps, Sequences, Tool Use, Technology Use) Skills are abilities developed through deliberate systematic effort, intentional practice and often supported by training and coaching.

Character (Honor, Morals, Ethics, Standards, Right/Wrong, Dependability, Attendance, Promptness) Character is keeping commitments, agreements and striving for excellence.

Collection - Other Strengths (Geography, Chronotype, Climate, Seasons, Pace, Spiritual Gifts, Experience, School, Bandwidth, Thinking Style, Tools, Tribe, Adversities, Disabilities) A strength is any resource, internal or external that can be turned into a marketplace contribution.

DREAM JOB!!!

Strengths Summary

Contribution		

Passion	Talent	Personality
Values	**Learning Style**	**Knowledge**
Skills	**Character**	**Other**

Target

1. Professional Objective - What you want to "Do".

2. Target Market Statement – Where you want to "Do" it.

3. Target Industry/Company/People List – Who can hire you?

4. A-B-C-D Sequence

    Any Job –

    Better Job –

    Career Job –

    Dream Job -

SUCCESSPATH C21 Resume Review Checklist

Credentials - Do I have the majority of qualifications the company requests in the job description?
  Do I have the education or substitutions required?
  Do I have the experience requested?
  Do I have the skills and baseline competencies requested?

Customized - Is my resume targeted to a specific industry for a specific company for a specific position?
  Have I chunked or deconstructed the job description?
  Have I identified the keywords?
  Have I used the keywords where I can honestly match the request?

Contact Information – Is my information current and professional?
  Does my location match?
  Is my phone number up to date?
  Is my voicemail cleared out?
  Is my message professional?
  Do I check my messages 3x daily?
  Is my email current and professional?
  Do I check my email inbox 3x daily?

Clear Targets – Does the resume clearly communicate the position being applied for?
  Does it use company specific language?
  Is my target at the top right under my name and contact information?

Contribution – Do I clearly communicate the value I could add at the position I'm applying for?
  Does my resume clearly quantify my accomplishments?
  Are my past contributions evidenced with numbers and statistics?
  Does my resume show evidence of specific results?
  Does my resume show evidence of earning money or reducing costs?
  Did I show evidence of meeting company goals?
  Did I show evidence of career progress?

Core Strengths – Does my resume have an easy to read list of my strengths?
  Have I listed my skills?
  Have I listed my technology proficiencies?
  Have I listed my traits?

Chronological Work History - Does my resume have a strong chronological component?
  Can the recruiter or hiring manager see my employment patterns?

Computer Reader Ready - Is my resume set up for Applicant Tracking Software?
  Have I used fonts that are likely to be scanned?
  Have I used a format that is likely to be scanned?
  If I'm attaching the resume, is my name clearly a part of the file name?

Compatibility – Is my resume in a software format being used by the company where I want to work?
  PDF?
  Apple Pages?
  Microsoft Word?
  Version? 1997-2003 is safest

Conservative-Creative Company Culture Continuum - Does my resume fit the company?
  Is the company/manager creative, contemporary and cutting edge?
  Is the industry/company/department/manager conservative?

Conventions - Are standard resume conventions and norms adhered to?
  Have all specific requests been observed?
  Have I used the first person simple with the imaginary "I"?

Convenient - Is my resume easy to read?
  Does the filename include my name and the position title?
  Have I used bullets, bold and caps to make information stand out?
  Is my resume uncluttered with plenty of white space?
  Have I used a single-word, short-sentence format?

Concise/Clockwise – Does my resume communicate in a 10 second reading?
  Is my resume one, two or three pages based on norms or requests?
  Is the resume written in a data dense style?
  Look at the resume for 10 seconds and circle what stands out.

Consistent - Is my resume consistent?
  Is my punctuation consistent?
  Is my number usage consistent?

Corrected or Critiqued - Is my resume free of errors?
  Did I run spell check?
  Has someone else looked at the resume for grammatical, punctuation and spelling errors?

Clean, Crisp Copies - Do I have copies to bring along for the interview?
  Is the resume on resume paper? Are the copies clean and crisp?

Complete - Does my resume follow the C.A.R.E.E.R. or some other proven model? Does my resume have all the pieces in an order that makes sense for my industry?

Cyber Safe – Am I limiting information like my physical address?

Contemporary – Does it reflect up-to-date thinking and tools?
  AOL emails suggest age
  WordPerfect suggests age
  File Maker Pro suggests age

Connected – Does my resume display links to outside resources?
  Does it link to my email?
  Does it link to my *LinkedIn* page?
  Does it link to a website, blog or work sample?

Collection – Do I have a package of resume deliverables?
  Position Description Deconstruction?
  Resume?
  Application Master?
  Cover Letter?
  Reference Sheet (People to Call)?
  Reference Letters?
  Endorsement Sheet (Comments on Your Great Work)?
  Leave Behind with Qualifications Match?
  LinkedIn Profile?
  Thank You Note Sequence?
  Portfolio Work Samples (Paper, Digital-PowerPoint or Online)?

Bonus

Courier – How am I getting my resume in the hands of a hiring manager?
  Personally handing to them?
  Company insider personally handing it to them with a reference?
  Leaving it with their assistant?
  Mail?
  Email?
  FedEx?
  Courier Service?
  Western Union?
  Applicant Tracking System?

Interview Question Review

Position Description Qualifications	Tell Me About Yourself	Why Are You Interested In The Position?
Greatest Strengths	Weaknesses	Co-Workers Say
Work Irritations	Achievements	About Company
Goals	Questions for Me Average Work Day? Traits of Success? Appropriate Dress? Training Program? What should I ask?	Interest Statement Based on what you've said, I think I would be a good fit. What is the next step? May I have one of your business cards?

Interview Checklist

Cell Phone Is In The Car
No Gum

Arrive 20 Minutes Early - Go In 10 Minutes Early

Use Bathroom Somewhere Else

Bottled Water/Energy Bar/Caffeine (leave in car)

Toothpick or Brush (leave in car)

Breath Mints (leave in car)

Advil or *Aspirin* (leave in car)

Directions (The GPS System Doesn't Always Work Perfectly)

Cash (For Parking, Tolls and Emergencies)

Worst Case Scenario Kit (Spot Remover, Umbrella, Band Aids)

Your Interview Kit (Items to Bring In)

A Nice Portfolio Style Binder

Samples of Relevant Work

Printed Copies Of Your Resume x3

Pad & Paper

Pen - 3x

A List of Job Related Questions

Reference Sheets

Copy of Cover Letter (If Sent)

Copy of Job Description

Copy of Job Description Deconstruction

Strengths Based Job Search Review

Set Up
1. Professional Communication-Cell Phone & Gmail
2. Transportation-Housing
3. Professional Image/Wardrobe

Stand Out Strengths
1. Passion Based Knowledge
2. Talent Based Skills
3. Market Based Contribution Statement

Target
1. Professional Objective – What you want to "Do".
2. Target Market Statement – Where you want to "Do" it.
3. Target industry/Company/People List – Who can hire you?
4. A-B-C-D

Resume
1. Modern Resume & Cover Letter
2. References & Recommendations
3. Portfolio

Interview
1. Written Talking Points
2. 10 Questions
3. Tell Me About Yourself

Direct Contact
1. Hidden Job Market
2. Contacting Hiring Managers
3. Information Interviews

Employer Posts
1. Online Application
2. *Indeed*
3. *Craigslist*

Relationship Networking
1. Refer-ability Habits
2. *LinkedIn* Profile 25
3. Conferences, Industry Groups, Meet Ups

Staffing & Search Firms
1. Sign Up
2. Interview
3. Stay In Touch

Challenges
1. Identify
2. Manage-Solve-Leverage
3. Execute

***Agile* Job Search Planning**
1. *Kanban* Board
2. Sprint, Sprint Plan, Sprint Review
3. Sprint Retrospective.

www.ingramcontent.com/pod-product-compliance
Lightning Source LLC
Chambersburg PA
CBHW071405170526
45165CB00001B/183